11-21-84	Samuel	218
	Phillip Posey	
4-23-89	Maura H.	110
11-4-92	Maribel Delgado	B-18

978
M
c.1
McCall
Cowboys and cattle
drives

TALCOTT SCHOOL LIBRARY

FOREWORD

"Frontiers of America" dramatizes some of the explorations and discoveries of real pioneers in simple, uncluttered text. America's spirit of adventure is seen in these early people who faced dangers and hardship blazing trails, pioneering new water routes, becoming Western heroes as well as legends, and building log forts and houses as they settled in the wilderness.

Although today's explorers and adventurers face different frontiers, the drive and spirit of these early pioneers in America's past still serve as an inspiration.

ABOUT THE AUTHOR

During her years as a teacher and reading consultant in elementary schools, Mrs. McCall developed a strong interest in the people whose pioneering spirit built our nation. When she turned to writing as a full-time occupation, this interest was the basis for much of her work. She is the author of many books and articles for children and adults, and co-author of elementary school social studies textbooks.

Frontiers of America

COWBOYS

and CATTLE DRIVES

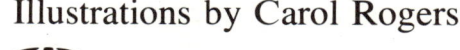

By Edith McCall

Illustrations by Carol Rogers

CHILDRENS PRESS, CHICAGO

978
M
c.1
645

Library of Congress Cataloging in Publication Data
McCall, Edith S
  Cowboys and cattle drives.
  1. Cowboys—Juvenile literature.
  2. Cattle trade—The West—Juvenile literature. I. Title.
PZ7.M1229.Co   64-19886
ISBN 0-516-03312-3

Cover photograph courtesy of the National Archives

New 1980 Edition
Copyright© 1964 by Regensteiner Publishing Enterprises, Inc.
All rights reserved. Published simultaneously in Canada.
Printed in the United States of America.
1 2 3 4 5 6 7 8 9 10 11 12 R 87 86 85 84 83 82 81 80

CONTENTS

Charlie Goodnight's Story
    GROWING UP IN TEXAS 9
    BLAZING THE GOODNIGHT TRAIL 25
    ADVENTURE ON THE TRAIL 46

James Cook's Story
    THE MAKING OF A COWHAND 61
    GREENHORN ON THE CHISHOLM 83
    INDIANS ON THE CHISHOLM 93

Tom Smith's Story
    TRAIL'S END MARSHALL 105

Will Rogers' Story
    LATER DAY COWBOY 117

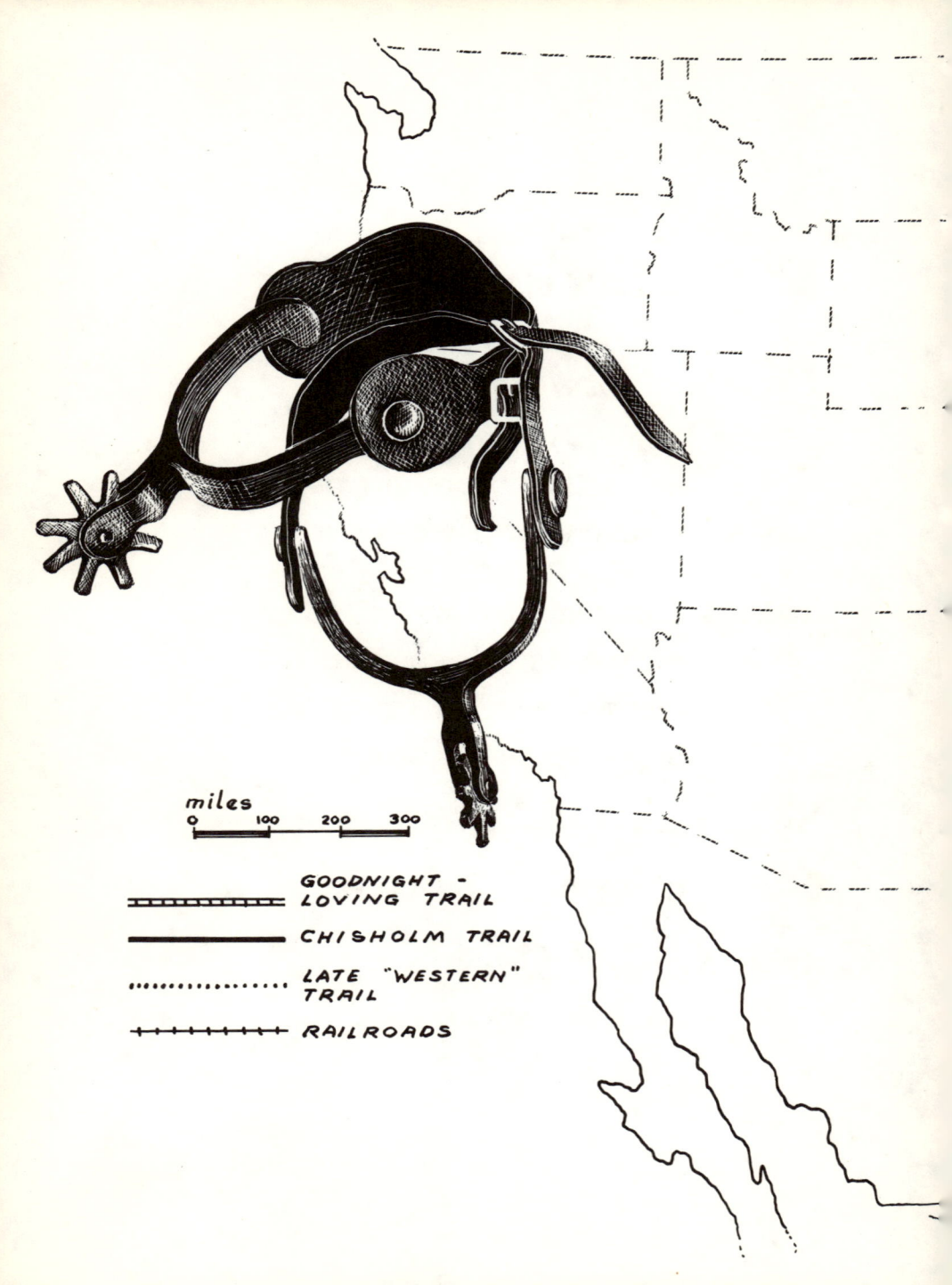

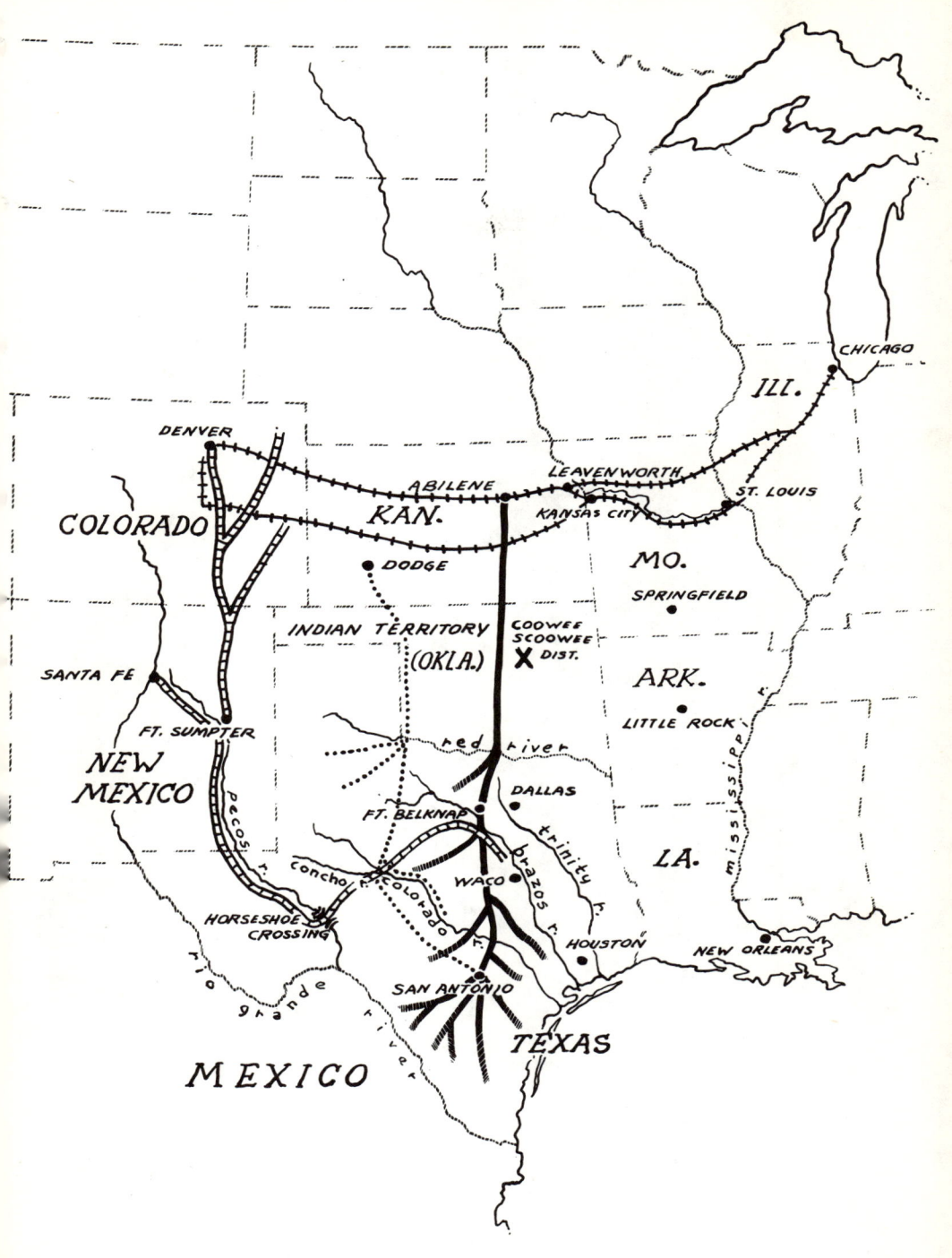

Charlie Goodnight's Story
GROWING UP IN TEXAS

Charlie Goodnight woke up very early on a certain morning in the fall of 1845. He looked for the last time at the split in the woodshake roof of his Illinois cabin home — the split that his stepfather had been <u>meaning</u> to mend for more than a year. Charlie saw the thin line of gray light coming through the crack and started to curl up into a tighter ball to sleep until his mother called him. He could hear her now, poking up a fire in the old wood range down in the kitchen.

He remembered then.

"Texas!" he said. He reached across to another curled up shape under the old quilt and gave it a poke. "Hey, Lije! Wake up! This is the day we start for Texas!"

That was the day Charlie Goodnight's life really began, although he was already nine years old, for Texas and he were to grow up together in the cattle business. That was the first day of many that Charlie was to spend on the back of a horse from morning until dark, and even into the night.

At day's end, on the first day on the trail to Texas, Charlie's thighs and back ached. He had ridden the family's white-faced mare, Blaze, all day with neither saddle nor blanket to ease the ride. But he did not mind, for they were twelve miles closer to Texas. The family was going there because Hiram Dougherty, Charlie's stepfather, had heard so much talk of the new state of Texas that he could no longer see anything good about his home and farmland on the edge of the Illinois prairie.

"Things grow tall in Texas," the talk went. "Corn and men, too. And they're practically giving away farmland. Any man can get rich there without half trying."

That sounded fine to Hiram, who had never really enjoyed hard work. On that fall day, when the oak leaves were turning red and brown and the hickory burned golden in the woods, Hiram happily clucked at the horses as he held the reins from the seat of one of his two covered wagons. Beside him was little seven-year-old Cynthia Goodnight and his wife, who had been the Widow Goodnight for a year before she married him. Elijah, thirteen, drove the second wagon, with his sister Elizabeth, who was eleven, riding beside him. Charlie, on Blaze, kept the cows moving along behind the wagons, with no idea that this was a job at which he would spend much of his life.

At that time, there wasn't a bridge anywhere across the Mississippi River. When the family reached the river after a few days, they had to wait at the gently sloping river bank until it was their turn to load wagons, people and animals onto the ferry boat.

As they waited, Charlie peered eagerly at the other shore.

"Golly, Lije, look at all the steamboats," he said. "St. Louis must be about the biggest city in all the world."

On the ferry, they drew near enough to hear the shouting and singing of the men who worked on the river-front docks, loading and unloading boxes and bales from the steamboats, and stacking the decks with wood for the boiler furnaces. Beyond the slope of the river front rose rows of buildings, some twice as high as any the Goodnight children had ever seen. Beyond the buildings were tree-covered hills.

Through those hills, over the new, rocky road to Springfield, Missouri, they journeyed then, day after day. The road led over and around hills, down into valleys of rivers and creeks. The fall rains had not yet come, and the streams were low enough for the animals to cross quite easily. Once in a while they had to go through water up to the wagon beds.

Then the horses, dripping and snorting, slipped and slid as they pulled the heavy wagons to the top of another hill. Going downhill, the wagons often skidded dangerously as they rolled too fast for the teams. After about two weeks, the family arrived in Springfield, a frontier town not yet fifteen years old. It had a large, grassy public square, with a little scattering of cabins nearby. The Goodnights camped near the new, two-story brick courthouse that stood in the center of the square.

"Why not stay here, folks?" they were asked. "Fine prairie land around here, new mill being built, mail comes in regular-like — and there's an awful lot of rough road between here and Texas!"

But Hiram's ears had been too well filled with the stories of easy life in Texas. Later, when the wagons almost fell apart on the mountain road through Arkansas, he wished he had stayed in Springfield. When at last they came to the flood plain of the Arkansas River, and crossed it on the ferry at the settlement called

Little Rock, people again urged them to stay.

"The worst of the journey is over now," Hiram said. "Soon as we get the wagons patched up, we're going on to Texas."

With new iron hoop tires to hold the creaking wheels together, the travelers headed southwest once more. At last they reached the Red River that marked the boundary between Indian Territory, as Oklahoma was called, and Texas.

"Hooray!" shouted the boys. "We're in Texas at last."

But on they went, still to the southwest. They finally reached the Trinity River, at Dallas. Dallas was only a trading post with a couple of cabins nearby, and a ferryboat which was used as a bridge instead of a boat because the river was so low.

When they topped the rise on the other side of the river, Charlie called out, "Lije, look at the buffalo!"

He pointed up the river, where hunters on horseback were shooting buffalo as they rode. With the help of their dogs, they had cut off part of a herd that made a dark cloud in the distance. The hunters picked off the frightened animals, one after another, and the great shaggy bodies fell with a thud. The beasts bellowed

loudly as they kicked and struggled to rise before death came to quiet them.

Charlie found this exciting. He had heard that the great wild beasts came to Texas as winter brought snow to their summer feeding grounds. They seldom came as far east as the Trinity River, however, now that so many people were taking up land in that part of Texas.

Next they saw a herd of wild mustangs, streaming gracefully along a ridge on the far horizon. Charlie looked down at steady old Blaze, and thought how exciting it would be to ride a wild horse like one of those.

Maybe he could catch one someday. . . .

"Will we live near here?" he asked Hiram when they made camp that night. He was pleased with Hiram's answer.

"Not much farther to go. The ferry man told me about a good farm we can rent for the season. It's down on the Brazos River."

Two days later they had found that farm, but the family did not stay there long. There was trouble when Hiram showed no interest in planning how they would make a living. Charlie's mother took the four children and a new baby that had come and moved farther up the Brazos, without Hiram. They settled about fifteen miles west of Waco, and Lije and Charlie became the men of the family. They went to the neighbors' farms to work, even though they were not very big or very strong. But as time went on, their slender bodies became tough as young hickories.

One day, Lije came home on Blaze, holding the bridle reins with one hand and his rope with the other. He was leading a frisky young colt.

"Want it, Charlie?" he asked. "Somebody shot its mother, and I found it standing by her body. No sight of the rest of the herd of mustangs. It's going to take a lot of care, but it might make a nice horse for you someday."

Charlie's eyes glowed. "You bet I want it, Lije! Gee, thanks!"

He spent the next days repairing the old corral so that his little horse could not escape. It had a look of wildness in its eye, and at first would not let either boy get near it. But Charlie had a way with wild animals, and before long the colt was coming to him to get the cow's milk he brought it.

Charlie remembered his wish, made when he had seen that first herd of mustangs. They were rather small, sturdy horses that came from those that had escaped from the Spanish explorers, perhaps as many as three hundred years earlier. The little colt was probably a descendant of some of those Spanish horses, but his ancestors had been wild for many years.

Charlie looked forward for the next two years to the time when his colt would be old enough to break to riding. When that day came, the horse was so used to Charlie being near him that he let the boy climb onto his back. Charlie had no saddle, so he had to learn to ride bareback. And then, faster than he got up, he was sitting on the ground, looking up at his horse.

"All right, if that's the way you want it, that's the way you shall have it," Charlie said. He got to his feet, dusted off his jeans, and suddenly he was on the mustang's back again.

Just as suddenly, he found himself in a sitting position on the ground of the corral. Dust flew in clouds around him, and his mustang was looking over the fence as if nothing had happened.

"We shall see who's going to be boss in this corral," the boy said. It took him ten more times on the horse's back, but the last time he jumped off instead of falling off. Bruised and sore, he went back to riding his

mustang the next day. After about a week, the day came when he could ride the pony out of the corral, down the road a bit and back home.

Lije was watching. "Looks like you've got yourself a horse, Charlie," he said.

Safely inside the corral, Charlie pulled to a stop. He patted the horse's neck and said, "Yes, sir! This is my riding horse from here on. He knows who's boss now."

Just then the horse turned his head quickly as if he understood what Charlie had said. Quick as a wink, his heels were in the air, and then down. Next second he was standing almost straight up on his hind legs. Charlie, taken by surprise, slid right to the ground.

Lije was laughing. And Charlie, looking up at his horse and seeing the animal's mouth wide open in an unusually loud whinny, was sure the horse was laughing at him, too.

"Why, you scamp!" Charlie said as he dusted himself off. He had noticed for several days that the horse looked around before throwing him, as though to make sure he was not jamming the boy against a fence. "It's a game, is it? Well, now, we'll see if I can just stay on your back like I was glued to it."

He worked with the pony until he could ride him

anywhere, any time, and rider and spirited mustang worked as one being. As he bent low over the horse's neck and let him run freely, he remembered the day he had first seen the herd of wild horses, and his longing to feel the joyous freedom of the mustangs. Now he felt it, and all the wide world of Texas seemed his.

Lije was already learning to ride herd on cattle for some of the neighboring ranchers, but he preferred the tilling of the land on his mother's farm, and the tending of dairy cattle.

"You can ride better than I can, Charlie," he said. "I'll see if Mr. Loving will let you take my place so I can help Ma here at home."

Charlie was fifteen years old, but very small. He weighed less than ninety pounds. But he was so expert with horses that a neighbor had had him break and train a race horse for him; Charlie had then ridden the horse as its jockey in a race. He had come in first. Mr. Loving was glad to have an expert rider, small though he was, and soon Charlie was riding herd.

One day, as he headed back home for the night, he heard the pounding of hoofs and saw the leaders of a cattle stampede coming toward him. He headed off the cattle, turning them to start the circling that cowboys used to end stampedes. In payment, the cattle owner gave him a homemade saddle.

"Now you look more like a cowboy," Mr. Loving said when Charlie rode in the next day. "It kind of worried me that you rode bareback."

"Why, Mr. Loving? I don't fall off any more," he said, keeping a close eye on his mustang to see that he was not up to his old tricks.

"No, but I kind of wondered what you were going to hang your rope on when you herd cattle to market for me, and have to take some other gear with you."

Charlie laughed. But he was glad to know that he was good enough as a cowhand to help drive cattle to market. That was the whole point of raising cattle — to get them to a place where they would be bought for meat and for the cowhide.

By that time, it was plain to see that cattle raising was to be one of Texas' most important industries. Cattle had come into the state long before, while it was part of Mexico. These were Spanish cattle, of all colors from coal black to spotted red and white. The first cowboys in Texas were Mexicans, taught at the Spanish missions to tend the cattle. They were called *vaqueros,* and much that Charlie was learning now had been passed on down to American cowmen from the *vaqueros*.

A couple of years went by and Charlie left the ranch to go west, riding herd on cattle with a freight wagon train. He learned how to tell when water was near, how to read tracks, how to take care of himself in the wilderness.

His mother had married again after a while, and Charlie had a new stepbrother, Wes Sheek, who was also interested in cattle. Wes heard about some very young cattle the two of them could buy. They were regular Texas longhorns, the breed that had come from the mixture of Spanish cattle with years of running wild behind them, and perhaps some of the English cattle the Americans had brought to Texas when they came there. The longhorns sometimes measured over seven feet from horn tip to horn tip, and had grown long of leg, too.

"Of course we can't figure on getting any money out of them for a couple of years, Wes," said Charlie. "There are 430 head now, and if we sell only some of them and keep some breeding stock, we can build up a good herd in a few years."

They took the cattle up to good grazing ground on the upper Brazos. Each animal was marked with the

CV brand, from the ranch they came from. Cattlemen let their animals feed and water where they wanted to, knowing that they could round them up later on and separate them from other cattlemen's stock. The land was all open range, which meant anyone could use it. No one built fences, except around a small planted field.

"Look them over, Wes," Charlie said as they saw their animals settle down to graze. "Good looking stock. That's the business I want to be in, Wes. Cattle raising is for me — gets you outdoors, on horseback, where a man ought to be."

But money had to be earned, and Charlie bought a freight wagon to haul goods up from Houston to the ranchmen of the Brazos River country. Then, as Indians attacked the ranchmen who were taking their buffalo hunting grounds for cattle range, the United States Army sent companies out to ride patrol. Charlie Goodnight became a scout for one of these companies. He had to leave it to Wes to check on the cattle herd, which was almost ready to begin to pay off a little. The boys thought they could take part in a cattle drive to market at New Orleans, or even out to California to help feed the gold miners when spring came again.

But the spring that came was the spring of 1861, and the United States was no longer united. Texas was one of the states that tried to leave the northern states. Soon both Wes and Charlie were in the Confederate Army. The cattle were left to take care of themselves.

Charlie, as he rode the Texas plains scouting for his company, thought often of how his herd must be growing.

"When this is over, I'll have a fine herd to drive to market," he thought. He didn't know what was happening back around the Brazos River country.

BLAZING THE GOODNIGHT TRAIL

Charlie Goodnight rode home from war on a spring day in 1864. When he had had a few hours to feel like one of the family once more, he sat down to talk to his stepfather.

"I figure our herd should have at least six thousand head of cattle in it by now," he said.

Mr. Sheek shook his head. "You should have that many, Charlie. But while you were away at war, there have been fellows around these parts rounding up all the unmarked calves and even the grown cattle. They put their own brand on them. Claimed they were mavericks, and there for anyone to take."

A "maverick" was what unbranded cattle were called after a Texas rancher named Maverick had trouble claiming his cattle which had not been branded and had mixed in with other men's herds.

Charlie was angry. "That's not right. A man goes off to fight for his country and comes back and has to fight his neighbors for what is rightly his. How could Wes and I brand our animals while we were away?"

He walked back and forth in the low-ceilinged room. He stopped in front of Mr. Sheek, pounding his right fist against his left hand. "Thieves! Just thieves. That's what they are!"

Each day, Charlie grew more upset. He learned other things. Texas was so full of cattle that the price had dropped. During the war years, herds had multiplied and no one had time to drive many to market. Now there was little or no market. The northern cities wanted cattle, but not from Texas. The Illinois farmers said Texas cattle brought ticks to Illinois. The bite of the insect poisoned the Illinois cattle, and thousands had died. Also, Indians and outlaw white men were roaming Texas freely, giving trouble to drovers who tried to take cattle to market.

When Wes came home, he was discouraged, too, and decided to get out of the cattle business.

"I'll buy out your share," Charlie offered. He had been thinking of how and where he might sell a good part of the herd. Wes took his offer, and Charlie got to work. The next step was to have a roundup. He hired some good cowhands, the Wilson brothers, and he and his neighbors who had been keeping their herds up the Brazos packed up for a big roundup.

The first step was to ride for many, many miles, in a wide circle. Each time cattle were found, they were driven nearer to the center of that great circle. The riders closed in, little by little, until at last all the cattle were gathered in a great herd.

Fires were built then and branding irons heated over them. The cowhands, expert in handling a lasso, watched first for young calves with their mothers. The calf was lassoed, its feet quickly tied, and then the brand of its mother was quickly burned onto its hide in a tough place over the hip bones. Charlie and the others had to agree on many of the larger animals as to whose they were.

A little later, some of the neighbors who had not joined the roundup said Charlie was stealing their cattle.

Very angry, Charlie had a fist fight with one of the men, until the man admitted he had no proof. Disgusted with some of the ways of the people around him, Charlie said he was ready to leave Texas. He began to get ready. One day, he bought an old army wagon. He had it rebuilt with iron axles to make it as strong as possible. He would hitch six yoke of oxen to it and be able to carry enough supplies to take him and his men over many miles.

When the wagon was ready, he took it home and called his mother to come out to see it.

"Look, Ma," he said as he lowered a panel on the back of the wagon. "How would you like to cook dinner with this rig?"

Charlie had planned and made the first chuck wagon known to have been used on a cattle drive. Until then, cattlemen had carried their own gear on horseback, cooking as trappers and hunters had done for many years in the open lands of the West.

Mrs. Sheek watched as her tall, dark-haired, weather-beaten son lowered a hinged narrow board that made a table leg.

"There's the kitchen table. See all the cupboard shelves?"

"And I know what you ought to have on them," Mrs. Sheek said.

When the chuck wagon rolled out on the drive a short time later, the cupboard had a jar of her sourdough in it, as did practically every chuck wagon from then on. Sourdough was a batter mixture that baked up into fresh biscuits. The cook always saved some of the

dough to which to add flour, water, salt, soda and a bit of fat. The "starter" helped the biscuits rise, and had to be kept at a warm temperature all the time. Later, cattle-drive cooks were even known to take the starter jar to bed with them to keep it warm on a cold night.

Charlie had rounded up some good hands and a string of fine cow ponies. One-armed Bill Wilson and his brother, Charlie, were among the best of the hands, and old buddies of Charlie Goodnight's.

"Where are we going to sell the beef?" Bill asked.

"I figure the best market now is in Denver, boys," Charlie answered. "All those fellows who have gone out that way to mine gold are going to have to eat, and they're too busy digging for gold to bother herding cattle."

"I'm quitting, right now," said one of the new hands. "I ain't going to be scalped by no Comanche. They're thick between here and Denver, and all on the warpath." He picked up his gear, saddled his horse, and rode away. Another hand did the same thing.

"How about that, Charlie? How are we going to miss the Comanches and the Kiowas and get the herd through?" Charlie Wilson asked.

"By not going through their part of the country,"

said Charlie Goodnight. "We'll start out by going southwest."

"Southwest to go to Colorado?" The men looked at Charlie as if he were crazy.

"Sometimes the longest way around is the shortest way home," Charlie answered.

Bill Wilson shrugged his shoulders. "I don't mind how long the trail is as long as I get to its end with my hair still on my head." That was the way the other men seemed to feel, too. As for the men who quit, Charlie was glad to get rid of such men before he had to count on them to get him through a tough spot.

When they were alone, Charlie showed Bill Wilson a map of the trail they would follow. He planned to go southwest until they hit the old Butterfield Overland Mail route. This they would follow to Horsehead Crossing, on the Pecos River. They would follow the Pecos northward through New Mexico — northward to the gold fields of Colorado.

Bill grunted. "It's twice as far as the other way, Charlie. But maybe you're right. Only thing that bothers me is, how you going to get all those slow-walking animals across that desert?"

Charlie had hoped Bill would not think of that. It

was the part that worried him, too, but he did not want to admit it. He just said, "I reckon we'll make it all right, Bill. No other way, far's I can see, excepting right through the Comanche and Kiowa land. And you know that if we got through that with our hair still on our heads, the Indians would see to it that we didn't have a head of cattle left for all our bother."

So they began the long march. The first day, they reached Oliver Loving's camp, where he had been branding cattle. Charlie stopped to talk with his old friend.

"How about letting me go with you, Charlie?" Mr. Loving asked. "I've got my cattle all rounded up. The two of us ought to make it across that desert together better than alone."

Charlie put out his hand. "Let you? I'd like nothing better!"

So they agreed to travel together. Charlie felt much better, for there was no better cattleman than Oliver Loving. He had been handling cattle twenty years longer than Charlie had, and had taught Charlie Goodnight much of what he knew. Further, Charlie admired and liked Oliver Loving.

Soon Mr. Loving's cattle and men were with Charlie's

on the trail. Charlie rode ahead as much as twelve or fifteen miles each day to check the trail and find the watering places for the herds. Mr. Loving rode with the herd as trail boss, bringing up the rear. Two good cowboys led the way shown by Charlie's trail. The rest were spread out along both sides of the great mass of longhorns.

Charlie, riding alone, watched for the signs of water he had learned in his days of scouting the West. He looked for the kind of swallows called mud-daubers as one sign. They flew low enough for a sharp-eyed scout to tell if they had mud in their beaks or not. Mud meant the swallow had just come from water. Dry mouthed, it probably was going toward water. Doves seen flying near were a hopeful sign of water, for they could not live long without it.

When a scout saw a herd of mustangs, he was sure to be near water. Charlie knew that if the horses were walking in a long line, they were more than likely going toward water. If they were scattered and stopped often to graze, they probably had just come from a water hole or river. Certain types of plants were signs to Charlie, too.

All had gone well as the herd drew near the Concho

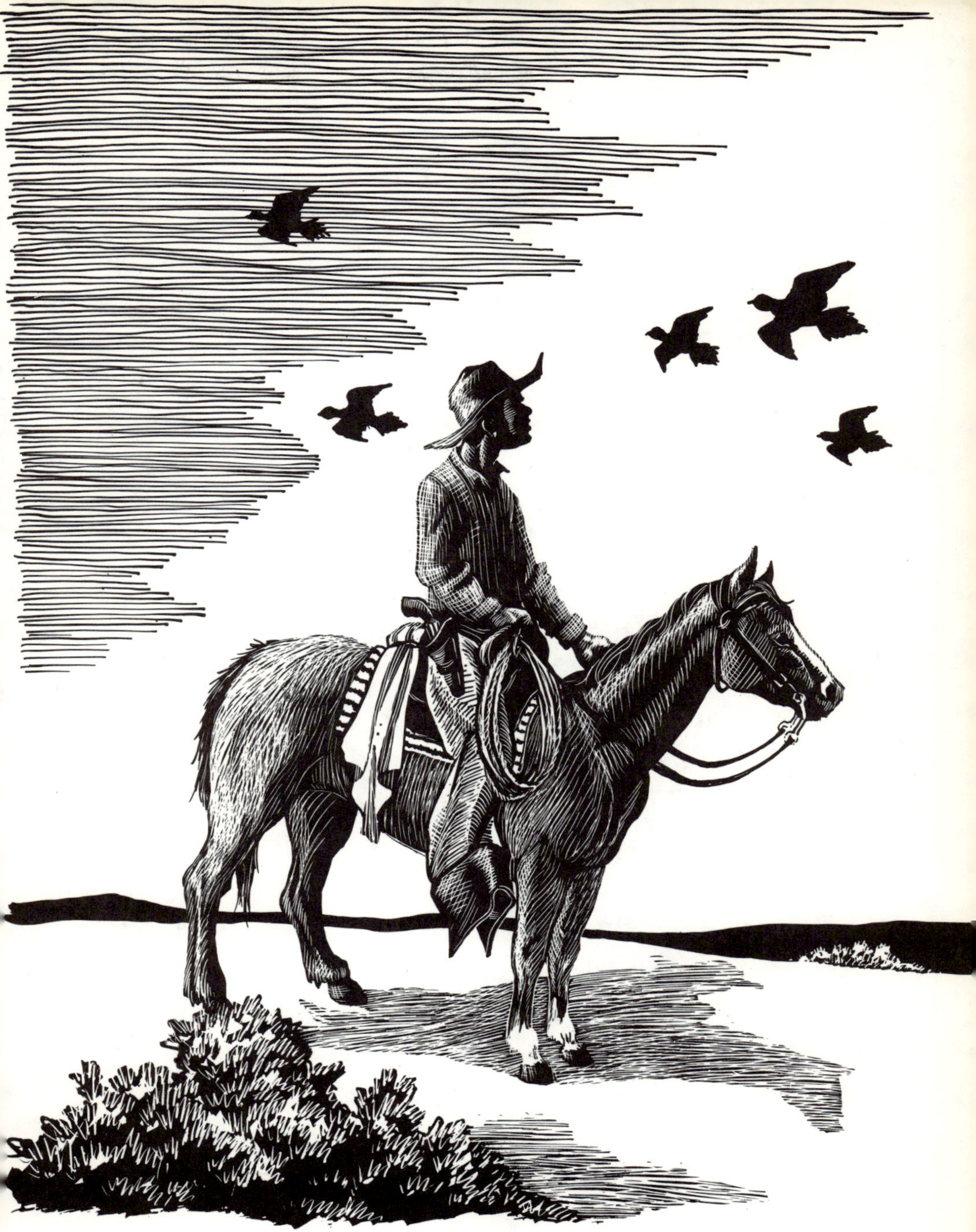

River, a branch of the Colorado which was the last watering place before the eighty-mile stretch of desert.

"How are we going to manage that desert crossing, Charlie?" asked Mr. Loving. "The cattle can't walk for six days without water. That's about how long it will take to go eighty miles."

Charlie said, "I think we should just move the herd along as fast as possible, in the hope we can make it before thirst drives them half crazy."

So they let the animals drink all they would, filled the canteens and water barrels and left the Concho late in the afternoon. They kept the animals traveling until well after dark, and were on their way again at dawn. When darkness came, they had made about fifteen miles. They stopped for the night.

Bill Wilson came riding up to Charlie about midnight.

"We can't get them to settle down. They're too restless because of thirst," he said.

This was not news to Charlie. It already was worrying him a great deal. Because the cattle were lowing and trying to break away from the herd to look for water during the night, most of the eighteen men were on horseback all night, and there was little sleep for anyone.

Charlie talked to his partner. "Mr. Loving, with all the walking the cattle have been doing in the night, they might as well have been following the trail. It takes no more strength to walk westward than in circles. I think we should stop trying to make camp at night and just keep moving."

Oliver Loving said, "I believe you're right, Charlie. We'll try it."

As the men and animals plodded onward that day, and the next and the next, the hot sun seemed to draw every last drop of moisture from their bodies. The air was stirred up by the thousands of hoofs into a white, bone-dry dust, making skin and cracked lips feel worse. The animals seemed to grow thinner each hour. Ribs stood out and skin pulled tightly over bony flanks. Tongues hung out and eyes grew bleary and sunken. More and more often, one of the cattle bellowed wildly, ran crazily from the herd and then back into the herd, trying to fight another animal.

Quickly then, before a stampede should start, a rider galloped forward, swung his rope, cut the animal from the herd and drove it away. There was no use trying to keep an animal gone crazy with thirst.

The herd strung out over more and more ground as the animals weakened. Mr. Loving rode at the very end with the "drags," urging them onward.

At the end of the third day, the cook drove the chuck wagon ahead of the herd and then stopped to build a fire. He used the last of the water in the barrels to make some coffee. As each man rode up to him, the cook handed the cowboy a tin cup of it, black and strong, to help him stay awake in the soothing, cooling darkness. On they went, but by now the cattle were hardly able to move one foot ahead of another.

Suddenly, at about two in the morning, there came an uproar.

"Baw-aw-aw-aww! Moo-OO-UNH!" and with the bawling there was the pounding of hoofs. The breeze was coming from Castle Canyon, where the dampness of night had settled, gathering whatever moisture the air held. The cattle, thinking there was water there, stampeded with the little strength they had left. The men rode as swiftly as their worn horses would carry them to bring the leaders into control. From each side, they closed in on the cattle, turning them back into the herd, until all were milling about. They held them there until dawn, circling, circling, circling endlessly.

As dawn came, Charlie talked to the riding men. "Look, boys — this is the last day of it. The Pecos is just twelve miles ahead. You'll need a drink yourselves to control the cattle when we draw near. Give me your canteens. I'm going to ride ahead and fill them."

With twenty canteens strung over his shoulders, Charlie mounted his least worn horse and urged the animal westward. As the horse at last caught the scent of water, he no longer needed urging. He rushed with a new burst of strength, but Charlie almost had to fight him to keep him from killing himself. He wanted to swing off the trail to a pool not far from the river, but the pool had such poisonous water standing in it that the horse would not have lived to carry Charlie back to the herd.

"On, boy — there's good water just ahead," he said as he forced the horse onward. Then there it was — Horsehead Crossing, where the Butterfield Mail coach regularly crossed the Pecos. The river began in the Rocky Mountains in northern New Mexico, flowing southward along the edge of the mountains' eastward ridge, on its way to join the Rio Grande.

Man and horse drank eagerly. Charlie was afraid

the horse would drink too much too fast.

"Not too much now, boy. You'll be back here soon," he said, and staked the horse back from the river while he filled the canteens.

On the way back to the herd, Charlie planned a way to lead the herd so that the breeze would not reach them from the pond before they caught the breeze from the river itself. He pulled a few hairs from his horse's neck and let them float on the breeze so that he could know the exact direction of the wind. Then, refreshed from his drink of water, he hurried back to give the men their full canteens. Spirits rose as soon as the men saw him.

Charlie spread the word then to move the cattle along, but to be careful to keep them following the way Charlie showed them.

"Charlie and Bill Wilson, and you, Dick and you, Sam, lead the way with me, and be ready to head off any cattle that might try to get to that pond."

On they went. As soon as the cattle were safely past the poisonous pond, they caught the scent of the river water. Then it seemed as if they suddenly went wild. They rushed headlong into the river, but the men made them move on to the other shore as soon as they had had a little water. They drank as they swam. Then once again they let them turn back into the river to drink, but not for long. They drove them to a grazing place not far away, but quite close to the pool of bad water.

"Now I've got to go back and give the rest of the men and Mr. Loving a hand with those that are still coming," Charlie said. "You fellows ride herd here. The cattle shouldn't drink any more for a while."

Then he took a second look at his men. All of them were nodding in their saddles from the many hours without sleep.

"Charlie, you stay awake and watch the cattle while these fellows get a ten-minute nap. We'll need you as soon as the rest of the herd arrives. Mind you now, keep an eye on these animals."

"Yeah, boss," said Charlie Wilson. His voice had a faraway sound. The rest of the men were already asleep sitting upright on their horses.

When Charlie had gone about one hundred yards he looked back. Six cattle were heading for the poisonous pond, and all four of the drovers were sound asleep.

Charlie gave a quick pull on the reins and swung

his horse around. "Cut them back, boy!" he said as he dug his spurs into the horse's side.

Horse and man did their best to cut off the cattle from the pond before they drank. But three of them were already drinking as he reached them. He awoke the men with his shouting, and looking a bit foolish, Charlie Wilson rode down to get the cattle back. Within a few minutes, the three cattle were lying on the ground. All three died.

About five hundred head of cattle still had to reach the river. The wind changed, and the smell of water reached them sooner than it had reached the others. Weak as they were, they, too, went crazy in their hurry to get to water. They rushed toward the river, not following the trail, but cutting overland the shortest way.

"Head them off! They'll kill themselves!" shouted Charlie. The cattle were not heading for Horsehead Crossing with its gently sloping banks, but for a place where the banks were steep. The men did their best, but they could not turn the maddened animals.

Without stopping, they rushed headlong for water, tumbling down the steep banks, leaping, scrambling.

Such a bawling was never heard before. The water churned and cattle bumped against each other, too crazed to have any sense about trying to save themselves. The herders saw many of them go under, not

to come up again. They forced their tired horses to try to make the cattle go toward Horsehead Crossing so that they could get them out of the river, but there was quicksand to watch out for, and some of the cattle got themselves under over-hanging bluffs where the horses could not get to them without being lost themselves.

"The Pecos — graveyard of the cattleman's hopes," Charlie Goodnight said later, remembering how the cattlemen had tried for two days to get some of the cattle herded and how many they had had to leave in the river, either dead or alive.

But he had learned what not to do on this first drive.

"If we ever do this again, Mr. Loving," he said to his partner, "we'll figure a faster way to get the cattle to water, before they go crazy. There must be a better way to do it."

He thought much about this as they headed the cattle up the west bank of the Pecos toward good grazing country. Except for this dry stretch, the new trail he had blazed for cattle herding was fine. He would not let this problem stand in the way of using the Goodnight Trail again. By the time they reached good grazing country and the cattle began to look fat again, he thought he had the answer.

ADVENTURE ON THE TRAIL

"Mr. Loving, I have a plan," said Charlie Goodnight as nine of the men sat resting near the chuck wagon. It was the Fourth of July, and the cook had given them the best possible cow-camp dinner. Everyone was feeling fine.

Mr. Loving's eyes were closed. "What is it, Charlie?" he asked without opening them. He was pleased with the way his young friend had grown into a man of strength; Charlie never seemed to wear out. He made a good partner for an older, wiser man who knew cattle and could give good advice but wanted to slow down a little.

Charlie said, "You can handle the drive from here on, Mr. Loving. There is plenty of water and grass because of all the mountain streams that run down to the Pecos from here on to the Denver mining camps. In the meantime, I'll hustle back to Texas and round up another drive. You can sell these animals as you see fit while I am gone. That way, I can bring another few thousand head west before winter sets in."

"You mean you can face that desert trip again?" Oliver Loving asked.

"Sure. I've figured out how to get those cattle across in less time, before they go crazy with thirst," said Charlie.

So it was settled. Charlie saddled up for the seven-hundred-mile horseback ride back to Texas. Mr. Loving went on to the north and laid out what was later called the Loving Trail. While Charles Goodnight was going east over the Goodnight Trail, Mr. Loving was finding buyers for the cattle. He sold the cattle sooner than he had expected to, to a western ranchman who wanted to fatten them on his big new ranch. Mr. Loving learned that Charlie had been right about the best cattle market for those years being in the west. Miners paid very high prices for meat. Supply camps were willing to buy cattle to hold for later sale, too, and new, growing cities such as Denver needed beef. There were also new ranchers who wanted Texas cattle to build up their herds.

Charlie, in the meantime, was making record time over his trail. He bought more of Texas' plentiful supply of beef cattle and trailed them westward. Mr. Loving and his hands met them just before the Horsehead Crossing and helped get the cattle across. This time the animals were not so hard to handle.

"What did you do, Charlie?" Mr. Loving asked.

"I saved two days, Mr. Loving. I let the cattle drink all they wanted at the Concho, and graze until noon, so that their stomachs were really full. We left the Concho then, stopped for a while at sundown for more grazing, and then on we went, all the way. With full stomachs, the animals trailed better and we saved those two last, hard days, and had less trouble with strays and drags."

"Good," said Mr. Loving. "I know just where we can sell this herd, too."

When all but the thinnest of these animals had been sold, the men found they had made twelve thousand dollars.

"Whee! Never thought we'd do that well," Charlie said. "But it may not last. While I was back in Texas I heard a couple of fellows say they thought they'd follow my trail and get in on this."

Mr. Loving grunted. "What's more, Charlie, the Comanches will begin to swing over this way. We've been lucky so far, but it may not last."

Charlie said, "Well, why not get in another herd before winter? If we can't get them all the way to market, at least we will have them here for the winter and will be first in to market in the spring. What do you say?"

"You willing to trail all the way back again?" Mr. Loving asked.

"Sure," said Charlie. "I'll take this money and invest it for us and both of us will be rich come spring."

"All right, if you can take all that hard riding, Charlie. I'll tend our herd here."

So Charlie got ready for the third trip of the season. He took three good men with him. Each one rode a saddle mule instead of a horse because mules could take the trip better, even though they were not quite as speedy as horses. Each led a fast horse to use in case of Indian attack, for it was rumored that there were war parties near. In addition, they took one pack mule to carry the supplies. Under the bacon and flour and coffee and cooking things was the tightly-tied, precious package holding the twelve thousand dollars.

As Charlie left, Mr. Loving gave the pack mule a slap to start him off. "Mind this fellow well, Charlie. He's a very valuable animal."

Because they did not want to lose everything in an Indian attack, the men hid in the daytime and traveled at night. Charlie led the way, with his saddle horse and the pack mule behind him. The cowboys followed, on their mules and leading their horses. They took turns standing guard at night while the others slept.

All went well until one night when they were almost down to Horsehead Crossing, down in the country near Carlsbad Caverns where traveling in the dark was hard, and a mule or horse could easily make a misstep. Charlie saw lightning off on the horizon, and felt a sudden gust of wind. Tumbleweeds and dust came driving at them, making horses shy and whinny in fright and men duck their heads to be able to go on.

Charlie turned. "We'd better find a place to sit this out, boys!" he called.

But before they could find any kind of shelter, the storm was upon them. They had no choice but to try to keep moving. Lightning flashed all about them, and rain fell in an almost solid downpour.

Charlie had his head bent low to break the drive of the storm. Suddenly the pack mule brayed loudly as a loud clap of thunder followed the crackle of lightning. The next instant, he was running full speed ahead, his rope flying after him.

"Mind the horses, boys!" Charlie shouted. He took

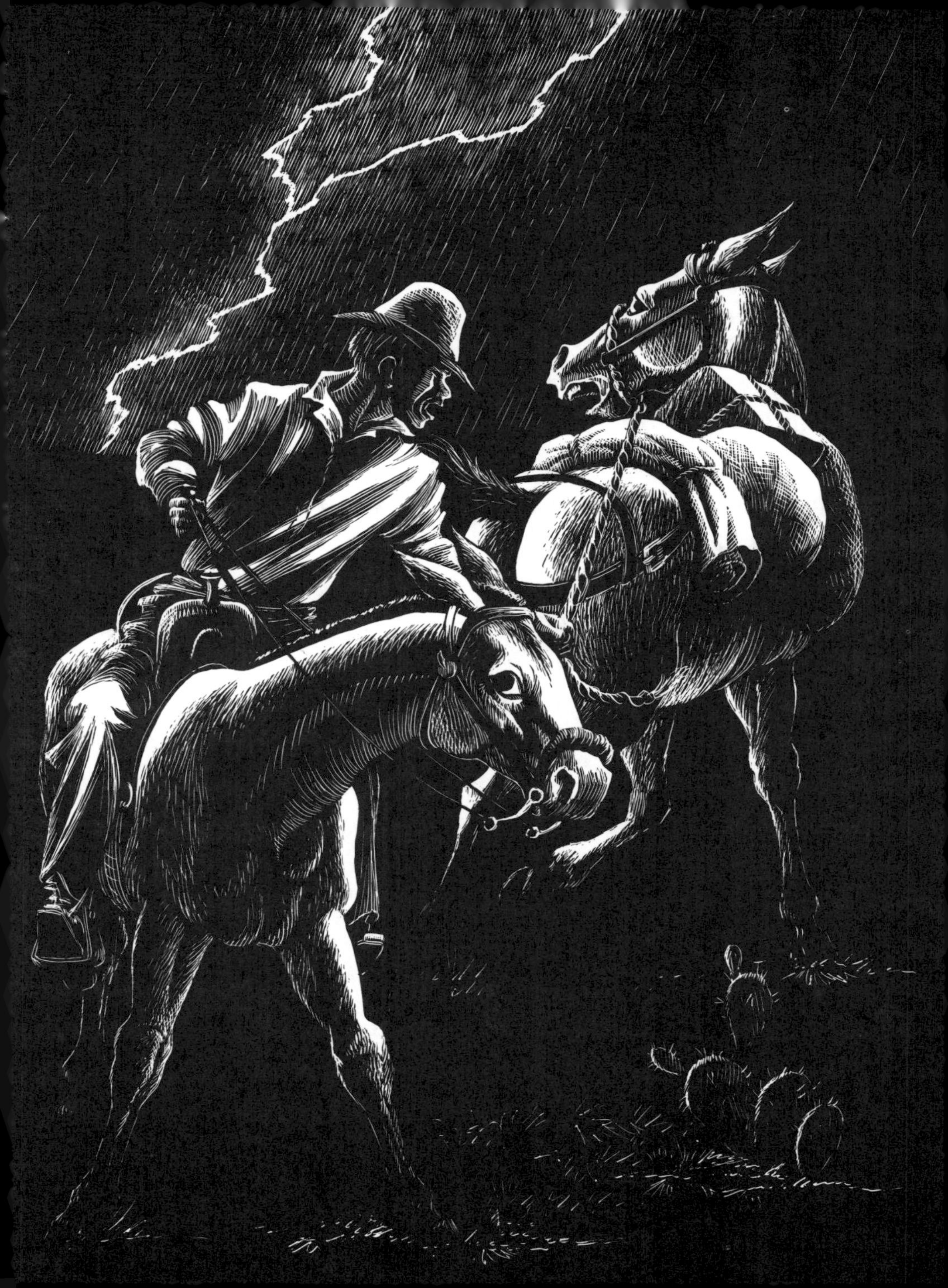

off after the pack mule. If the animal got away, the whole twelve thousand dollars would be gone with him, as well as the food supply for the rest of the journey. Charlie dug his spurs into his mule's sides and the animal stepped out at its fastest.

On went the chase in the darkness. The long-legged riding mule gained on the pack mule, and as lightning flashed, Charlie figured out just how he would catch the runaway. As the saddle mule passed the pack mule, Charlie leaped off, managing to get hold of the flying length of broken rope.

"Whoa! Whoa!" he cried, trying to dig his heels into the ground. "Whoa! Whoa, there!"

The mule nearly tore Charlie's arms from their sockets, for he tried to keep on running as fast as ever. He bucked and turned as Charlie let his weight drag along the ground, heels digging trenches as the mule kept going. But the rope was around the mule's neck and the pull on it choked him so that he had to stop, but not until animal and man were both breathing hard and the ground was pretty well dug up.

When the animal was finally quiet, the sudden storm had ended, leaving the night in thick velvet blackness. Charlie felt for the pack saddle on the animal's back. It was still there, but there was no pile of supplies on it. Charlie felt a sudden sinking inside him as his hands groped for the feel of the precious package. The money — thankfully, he felt its lumpy shape under the oilskin wrapping, just as the other men reached him.

"He threw off all the supplies, boys, but the money is still here," Charlie said. "We'd better hunt around and see if we can find any of the food."

In the blackness, the men tried to find the bundles, but they could find none. Rather than leave them, they camped there for the rest of the night, hoping that daylight would show them where the supplies were. But when dawn came, all they found was one square of bacon.

"Looks like the coyotes got everything else," said Charlie. "We're going to be a mite thinner when we get to Fort Belknap, boys."

With empty stomachs, the cowboys began the long desert trip. There wasn't even a jack rabbit for them to shoot. They filled their canteens at the crossing and began the long, hot trip across the desert. Now they had to risk being sighted by Indians, for they knew they could not last the trip if they hid in the daytime and traveled only at night. So on they went, as fast as the mules and horses would go.

They were weak and discouraged. Charlie was worried. What good was all that money now? Had he brought these three men to starve in the wilderness that stretched ahead, all because he was greedy to get another herd to market? Then, as they drew nearer the Concho, another worry was added. On the horizon to the east there was the dark shape of something moving toward them. Indians? Death for all of them could be the only result. There was no place to hide. Neither men nor animals were in condition to run for it or to put up a good fight against a war party.

"Indians, sure enough," said one of the men. "Our luck sure is down on this trip."

Charlie stared at the moving shapes, trying to figure out why they didn't spread out in the way that riding Indians usually did when they sighted the enemy.

"Come on, Charlie. Let's not just stand here. At least let's try to move out of their path," the men urged.

"Wait a minute," Charlie said. "I don't think it's a war party. See—there's something solid in the middle."

The other men peered, too, against the blinding desert sun.

"You must have good eyes, Charlie," said Bill. "It looks like Indians to me. Come on, boys. Let's switch our saddles to the horses and at least try to make a run for it."

"All right," said Charlie. As they switched from mules to horses, he thought about the twelve thousand dollars. What could he do with it? He would tie it to his saddle — but what good would it do if all four were killed? And that was most likely what would happen. He transferred the sack just the same.

They were just about to let the mules go free when he stopped for one more look. There was no mistaking it now. The solid shape he had seen was a wagon.

"Hey, fellows! Hold it. Look again. Even you blind boys can see that isn't Indians. It's a freight wagon, pulled by an ox team, and traveling alone."

"Well, I'll be a three-legged cayuse if it ain't," said Bill. "Now what kind of a danged fool would be travelin' alone in this country?"

They waited. When the wagon drew close, they found they even knew the "fool" who was driving it. He was old Rich Coffee, from the settlements up the Concho River. He had a loaded wagon and a twelve ox team.

"Where you going, Rich, and what's in your wagon?" Charlie asked. He had known Rich for some years.

"Well, Charlie, I'm heading up to Salt Lake where the Mexicans are loading up with salt. I aim to sell them my watermelons and bring back a load of salt myself."

"What did you say you have in the wagon? *Watermelons?*"

"That's right, boys. Care to try a sample? You look a mite dry."

"Let us at 'em," said Charlie. "We're not only dry but nearly starved to death."

Charlie never remembered watermelons tasting better. The boys feasted and even gave some to the horses to eat. They bought all they wanted from Rich, and loaded the pack mule with all he could carry. Rich had some other supplies he could spare, too.

"Not much use your going up to Salt Lake this time of year, Rich," Charlie said between bites of juicy watermelon. "The Mexicans take their carts up there early in the spring and late in the fall, when the salt's easiest to get. Your melons will rot before the Mexicans get up there."

Rich looked a bit discouraged, but he went on any-

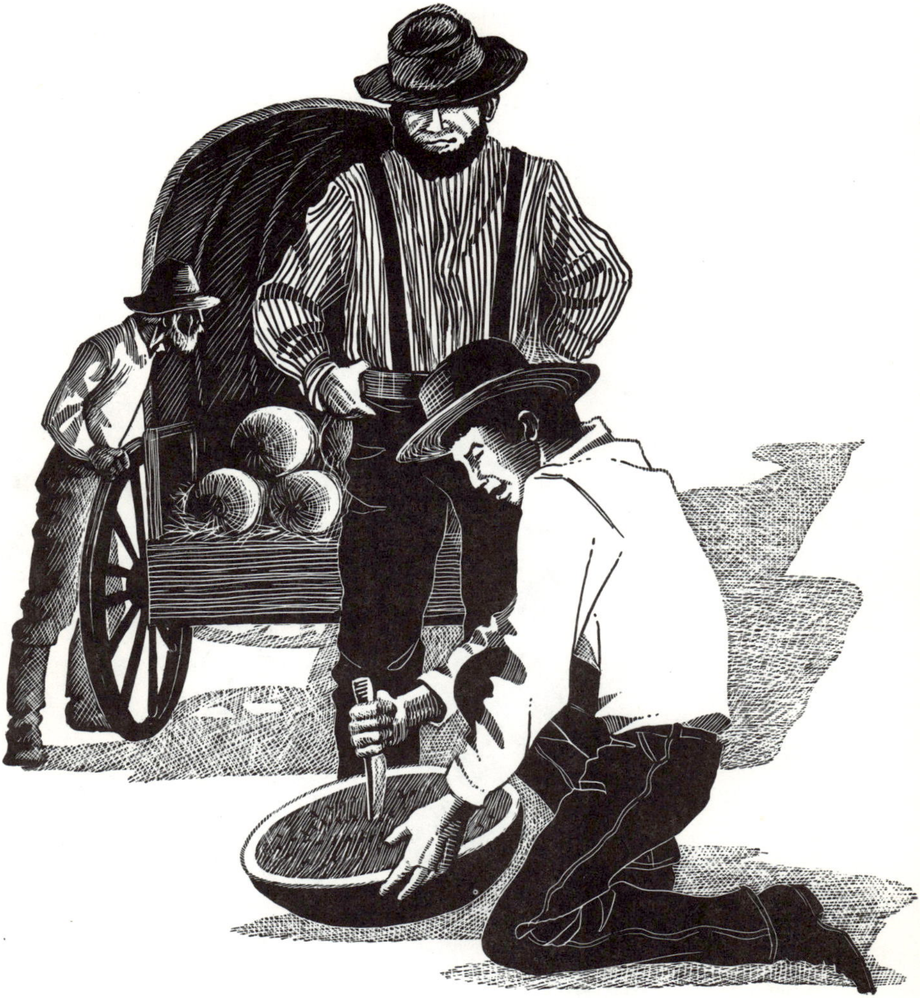

way, leaving some much happier cowboys behind him for his having passed that way. When Charlie next saw old Rich, the would-be watermelon merchant told him he had had to bury most of his melons in the sand.

The cattlemen reached Fort Belknap without meeting any Indians, and soon their journey was ended. They had made it in a record time of seventeen days, averaging forty miles a day. All four of them were grateful to Rich Coffee, and felt he had saved their lives.

Charlie wasted no time rounding up two-thousand head of cattle and enough cowhands to trail them back west. The greatest problem on the return trip came when they thought a herd of buffalo, crossing the trail as they headed south, would stampede the cattle. The herd was split into two parts, and for forty-five minutes the cowhands fought to hold them as the buffalo thundered between the two groups of restless cattle.

When at last the buffalo had moved on in a great dark mass, leaving a cloud of dust hanging over their wide pathway, Charlie anxiously rode back to see how many cattle had been lost. But his men had done their work well.

"Good riding, men!" he said when camp was made.

"If we lost enough head of cattle to count, I sure don't know where they're missing."

About forty days brought the herd to grasslands in New Mexico about forty miles south of Fort Sumner, not far from where Roswell, New Mexico, is now. Mr. Loving joined Charlie there, and they dug out shelters in the bluffs on the east side of the Pecos, making comfortable quarters for themselves and the men who chose to winter with them. There they kept the herd for the season, and because of this are said to be the first "ranchers" of New Mexico. Once a month they cut a hundred head of cattle from the herd and drove them to Santa Fe and Fort Sumner, to supply the army posts.

In the next years, the trails that Goodnight and Loving pioneered were traveled by many cattle herds, for other cattlemen soon learned of the western markets. Charlie himself liked the West so well that he opened a big ranch in Colorado, becoming one of the West's biggest cattle ranchers. Oliver Loving was not so lucky. The Comanches came to the new trails, as he had expected, and one day, when Mr. Loving and Bill Wilson were riding alone, the Comanches wounded him. By the time Bill could ride for help and Charlie

Goodnight reached his old friend, it was too late. The older man was dying. His name lives on in Texas and New Mexico, given to a county and a town, as well as to the trail up the Pecos.

Goodnight

Loving

James Cook's Story

THE MAKING OF A COWHAND

Stories spread all over the United States about the cattle of Texas and the adventures of the drovers who took the great half-wild herds to market. Up in the southern part of Michigan, a boy named James Cook went to the general store in the crossroads town as often as he could to listen to the talk of travelers.

Jim was thirteen years old in 1870. He was not very big, but he was an expert at splitting logs for firewood, swinging a scythe to cut hay, and especially at hunting small game with a rifle. He worked hard on the farm where he had been sent to live as an orphan boy at the age of two. But as he spent his days there in Michigan, he dreamed of going west. His head was full of adventure tales of buffalo hunters and cowboys.

"I'm going west next spring," he told his best friend. "I'm saving every cent I get for the furs I'll sell this winter. Then I'm going to Kansas."

"I'll go with you," said his pal, and by spring the two boys were ready. They took the train to Chicago and from there to Leavenworth, Kansas, which they had heard of as the place where Buffalo Bill had lived and gone to work on the wagon trains to the West. They took a cheap hotel room and began to look for ways to have adventures like those of Buffalo Bill.

The first day, when the bell rang for dinner, the boys took their places at the big table where all the hotel guests gathered.

"Have some of this good beef stew, boy. It'll put some meat on your bones," said the man who sat next to Jim. The man's face and neck were brown, and his eyes had wrinkles at the corners, as if he had squinted often in the sunlight. Jim helped himself to the stew, and soon was telling his new friend where he had come from and why he was headed westward.

"Thought I'd be a buffalo hunter," he said.

The man looked at the boy beside him. The lad was wiry, but nevertheless he was only about halfway to man size.

"Boy, one of those fifty-caliber buffalo guns would knock a little fellow like you down so hard you'd dig your own grave right there on the prairie. That's work for a grown man, not for a boy. No, about all a buffalo hunter would let you do now is skinning, and there's no fun in that. Just hard, backbreaking work."

Jim listened, a little disappointed at what he heard. "I'm real good with a rifle, sir, and I can ride well," he said.

"Then you ought to get work as a cowhand. See the West on the back of a cow pony. Get work with a Texas cow outfit. Now there's the place for a fine boy like you to do his stretching up to man size."

Jim and his friend talked over this idea and decided to go farther west on the railroad and look into it. Soon they were about halfway across Kansas, at Fort Harker. There they earned a little money helping ride herd on cattle grazing nearby while waiting to be shipped east on the railroad. To do this work, Jim bought himself a Comanche pony for fifteen dollars, and a good used Texas saddle for five dollars. He traded the pistol he'd brought with him from Michigan for a Spencer carbine, the short rifle the western cavalrymen at Fort Harker were using.

When the job ended as the herd of cattle was loaded into the slat-sided cattle cars, Jim had found his next job. "I'm going down to Texas with these fellows to work on a ranch. You want to come along? Maybe the boss can use you, too," he told his pal.

But the other boy was beginning to find the creak

of saddle leather a tiresome song. "No, Jim. I like it here. I'm going to work for a farmer, and homestead a place for myself as soon as I'm old enough."

So the boys parted. Jim rode out with the Texas cowhands early the next morning. Each man had his belongings rolled up and tied behind his saddle. All Jim had in his roll was a change of clothes.

When they had made camp in the open and eaten some bacon and cornbread, washed down with strong coffee, some of the cowhands got their blankets from the packs, rolled up in them and soon were snoring.

"You'd better turn in, too, Jim," said one of the men to the boy.

"Golly, Tom, I forgot to get a blanket," Jim said.

"That's all right. You've got a Tucson bed with you, same as I have," said Tom.

Jim asked, "A Tucson bed? What's that?"

"Easiest bed of all to make. Here's how you do it," said Tom. He stretched out on the ground, face down. "You just push your stomach onto the ground, like this. Then you cover it up with your back. That's a Tucson bed."

Jim found the "Tucson bed" very hard. He tried using his saddle for a pillow as some of the men did, but that, too, was uncomfortable. A tuft of grass seemed a better choice. In spite of the hardness of the ground he was too tired to stay awake, and so his first night in the open passed quickly. Before dawn they were breaking camp and on their way again.

Jim grew quite used to sleeping under the stars on his "Tucson bed" before they reached San Antonio. They were following the Chisholm Trail southward through Indian Territory and most of Texas. This was the route that a trader named Jesse Chisholm had pioneered. He used it first for his freight wagons as he went to and from his trading post in Indian Territory. Later, he drove herds of Texas longhorns up the same trail, and many Texas ranchers used it now for herding their cattle up to the railroad that ran through Kansas.

When they reached San Antonio, Jim was hoping they would go right on to the Slaughter ranches, but the cattlemen wanted to have a good time in the city before they went back to work at the ranch. Jim asked Mr. Longworth, the trail boss who had told him he thought Mr. Ben Slaughter might give him a job, how much farther it was to the ranch.

"About four days' ride, Jim. But we're in no hurry."

The gambling halls, dance halls and saloons where the men spent their time in San Antonio were not places a boy could go, so Jim spent his time loafing outside the buildings. There were many Mexicans around, and Jim tried to pick out Spanish words he heard over and over again. After a few days of this, he even tried saying a few Spanish words and found he could make himself understood a little.

At last the men had spent most of their money earned on the cattle drive from which they were returning. They were ready to head for the ranch, which was southwest of the town, not far from the Rio Grande River. On the fourth day they reached it, and Jim was shown to a bunk in a long shack that housed the ranch hands.

That evening, he saw a small man walking from the main house toward the ranch-hands' camp. Many of the men he had met were Mexicans and spoke only Spanish. Jim thought the man coming toward him was probably Mexican.

"*Buenas tardes,*" he said, showing off his newly learned Spanish.

The man was no longer young, but not much bigger than Jim himself. He wore the broad-brimmed hat, cotton shirt with a red bandanna kerchief, and trousers tucked into high boots that the cowmen wore. He had a well-filled rifle cartridge-belt over his hips, and a big butcher knife stuck into his right boot top. He stopped, looked Jim up and down for a long minute, during which Jim felt smaller each second. Then the "Mexican" said, in good English. "Yes, this is a mighty pretty evening, son. Now, tell me, who are you?"

Jim soon learned that this was Mr. Ben Slaughter himself. Mr. Slaughter offered him ten dollars a month and his board.

"But I'll expect a good day's work every day out of you, Jim. That is two dollars more than I pay my Mexican hands. Now I know you won't be worth a hoot until you learn how to rope a cow, but I think you have the makings of a good cattleman."

"Thank you, sir," Jim said. "I'll do my best to learn quickly."

The stars were still shining when Jim heard a banging on a pan and the cook's voice singing out,

"Roll out, on your feet!
Coffee's boilin', time to eat!"

The coffee was strong enough to make a man's hair stand on end. With it came thick salt-pork strips and slabs of coarse corn bread. Right after breakfast, Longworth and three ranch hands rode off to a pasture. They were soon back driving a herd of horses into the corral near the ranch house.

"You, Jim!" Mr. Longworth called. "Saddle up this pony for yourself," he said, pointing out a lively-looking but sturdy horse. "These others will be your string, too."

He showed Jim two other horses to which he was to change as his pony grew tired. Jim tried hard to memorize the markings on each, so as to be able to pick them out of the *remuda,* as the horse herd was called. Then he got his saddle and put it onto the first pony Mr. Longworth had pointed out.

"Going to show you how to cut an animal out of the herd. We're after a beef to butcher," Longworth told him.

"Yes, sir," said Jim. He pulled the cinch on the pony, and suddenly the pony jumped into the air, coming down with head down and heels flying.

"Whoa, whoa, whoa!" Jim yelled as he grabbed for the reins. He held onto them, knowing that every man on the place was watching to see how the greenhorn would handle this bucking bronco. Two bucks later

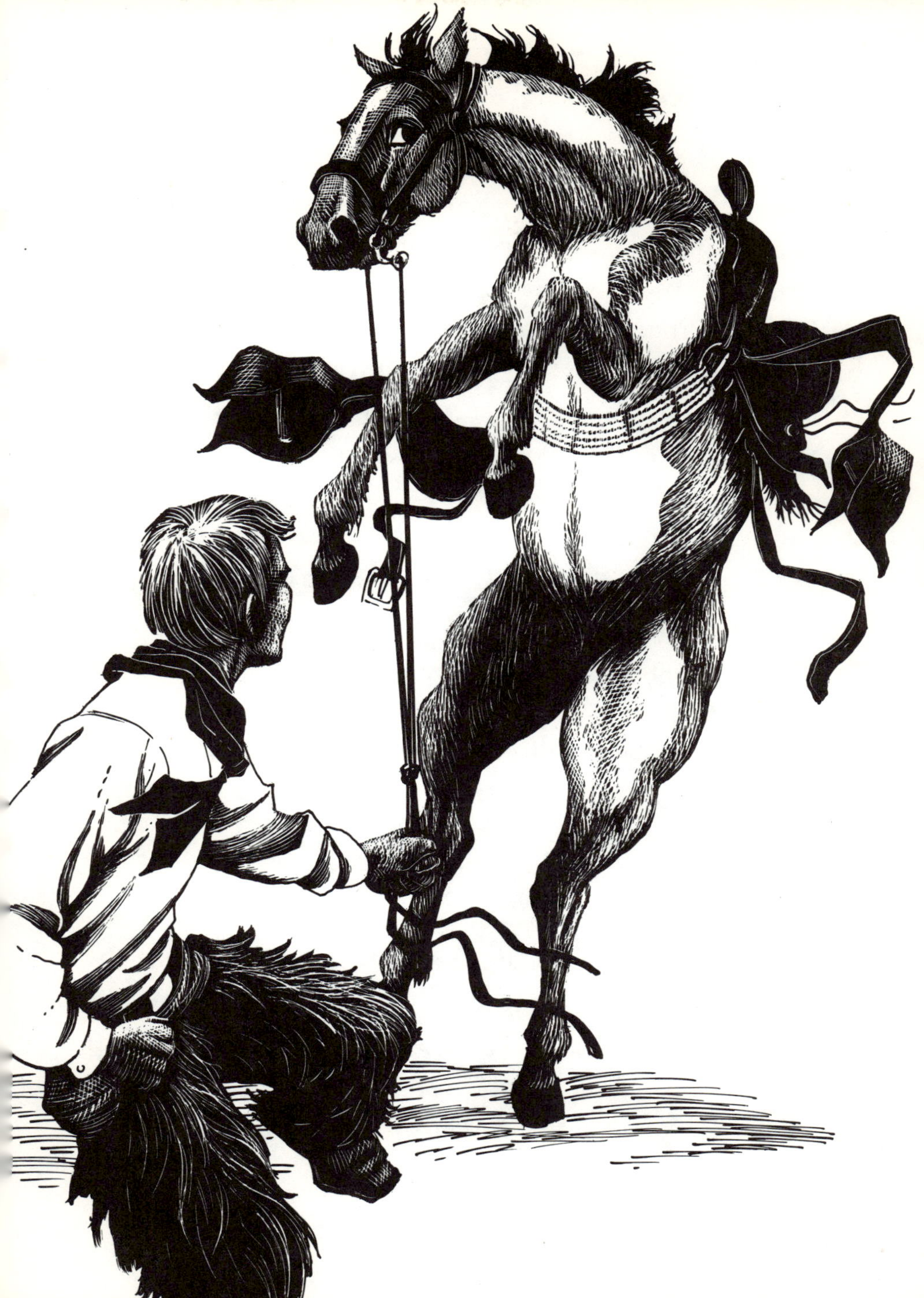

and he had his left hand on the saddle horn, and was half-seated in the saddle when the pony arched his back and jumped again. Somehow, Jim held on and got his feet into the stirrups. The pony bucked again and again. Then, as suddenly as he had begun to buck, he stood still and turned his head to look at his young rider, as if to say, "You're not the greenhorn I sized you up to be."

The cowhands were all grinning. Tom said, "Thought sure we were going to see you sun your moccasins, Jim."

Jim felt good as he took his place at the end of the line of riders that moved out of the corral. They rode down to a pasture, where longhorns milled about. They were tame cattle, Tom said, not because they were gentle, but because they were used to seeing men and did not immediately take off as the wild cattle did. Each of these animals was marked with the T-Diamond brand of the Slaughter ranch.

Jim watched the skillful way a couple of the cowhands and their horses separated one animal from the rest, the one Mr. Longworth had pointed out for butchering. Just as Mr. Longworth was aiming a shot at the animal, Mr. Slaughter came riding up. The shot hit the animal, but did not drop it to the ground.

It frightened the other animals, who came so close that Jim thought he was going to be run down. He soon saw, however, that his pony was trained to side step danger without being frightened by these bellowing beasts with the long horns.

"What's the matter with you, Longworth?" Mr. Slaughter shouted. Longworth had fired again, and still the animal did not fall.

One of the hands roped the wounded steer, but as the rope tightened it snapped. The animal was thrown, but it got to its feet, bellowing madly and charging right toward Mr. Slaughter.

Jim, near the ranch owner, snatched his rifle from the saddle holster. The steer was only six feet away when he fired right at its head, between the eyes, while Mr. Slaughter was trying to get his aging pony to move out of the way. The steer dropped instantly.

Mr. Slaughter's eyes as he looked at Jim said more than his words. He nodded briefly and said, "I reckon you'll do to help fight the Comanches, boy."

Jim watched as the Mexicans butchered the animal. Later, he had lessons from these descendants of the first cowboys in how to use the rawhide in making needed things, and how to dress and handle leather.

These men were experts at making harness, braided ropes, quirts, and even saddles. They could work strips into fine braids and knots, and tool and stitch handsome pieces from a piece of cowhide. Jim tried to learn, but he did not have the skill of these men. He liked to hear them talk, and added to his Spanish each day. He soon felt at home among these black-haired men with their cheerful grins.

That evening, Jim was issued his camp equipment. He was given a Mexican blanket, a tin cup and plate, and an iron knife and fork. He also had his own fine Bowie knife, which he had bought in San Antonio. On its blade was engraved, "Never draw me without cause, nor sheathe me without honor." He tried to remember those words later, when he learned how easily men got into fights on the frontier.

Early the next morning, Longworth and ten hands, including Jim, saddled up to go on a wild cattle hunt. Jim was surprised to find that they were to drive the tame herd from the pasture along with them.

"This is the decoy herd," Longworth said, but Jim had no idea what he meant.

Each man had his string of three or four ponies with him. There were also pack mules, to carry the supplies, for they were to be away from the ranch for several days.

About five miles from the ranch, they made camp near a big old corral that stood out in the open country. It was made of posts set on end in the ground, making a wall about seven feet high. The posts were lashed together with rawhide and crosspoles. There was a strong gate, and long wing fences reaching out from the gate, spreading farther apart away from the corral. This formed a wide opening, to help the men in herding animals into the corral.

Except for those needed to ride herd on the tame cattle, the men spent the rest of that day repairing and strengthening the corral. In the morning, Longworth led the way as the men herded the cattle along behind him. The grasslands were dotted with low-growing pines and oaks, the shrub called mesquite, and great prickly pear cactus plants, from one-foot high to the height of a man. About a mile from the corral, Longworth reached a dense patch of this growth. He signaled the men to drive the cattle into this scrubby woods.

"Hold them here," he ordered. "You, Carlos, and you, Pedro, stay with the herd. The rest of you follow me."

Jim wondered what this was all about. Not knowing what to expect, he held his pony until he could take last place in the line of riders. They rode for about two miles, through much the same kind of country. Jim often had to bend low to keep from being hit by tree limbs. Where the growth was thicker he had some trouble keeping the man ahead of him in sight.

"If I lose sight of him, I could wander around for days in this country," he thought.

Suddenly, there was a crashing sound ahead. Immediately, all the riders rode full speed, as if demons were after them. Jim had no choice. He had to ride full speed, too, for two reasons. First of all, he had to follow the others or be lost. Second, his horse was trained to this business, and immediately took after the horse ahead of him without any urging.

"Hey, watch out!" Jim yelled. The horse was taking the shortest route, even where there was barely room for him to clear the low limbs. Jim had to drop to one side to keep from being knocked out of the saddle. The next moment he had to get to the other side to clear a tree trunk.

Through the prickly pear, with its barbed thorns, under the live oak, crashing through mesquite shrub,

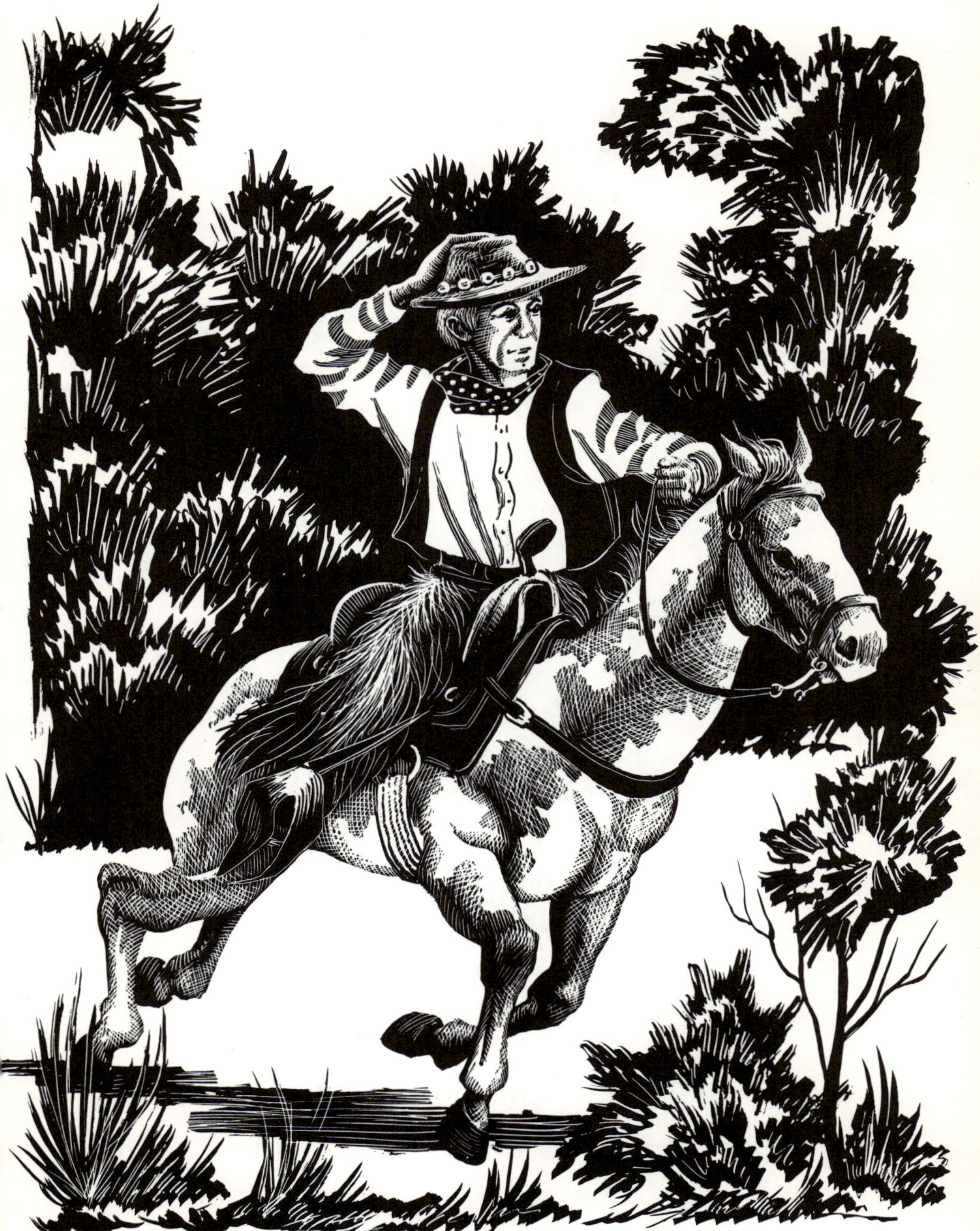

on the horse went. Brush swept across Jim's face. Heavy limbs scraped his bent back; thorns from the prickly pear stabbed him. He held on and hoped. Sometimes the cowpony tried to leap over prickly pear clumps, for he seldom wasted time by running around them.

Jim could only hold tight and wish for the wild ride to end. Then, just as suddenly as it had started, it was over. The cowhand ahead of Jim came into sight, his horse standing statue-still. Jim's pony knew what to do. He, too, stopped immediately and "froze" except for the heaving of his chest. The cowhand ahead pointed into the brush, and Jim looked to see what was there. He could see some cattle.

Then, for the first time, Jim heard the cowboy's lullaby, a strange crooning without words, sung to the cattle. Some said it was to let the cattle know a man was near, so that the animal would not be startled and run. Others said the weird singing was quieting to cattles' nerves. The men began to ride again, but now it was slowly, in a great circle. But each time around, the circle became smaller, and constantly the singing went on.

As he followed in the line of riders, Jim figured this thing out. They had ridden fast and hard after Longworth sighted the herd of wild cattle. When the cowboys were ahead of the herd, so that it was between them and the tame decoy herd, they swung around it and made the wild herd turn back toward the tame herd. This patch of brush was the one in which the decoys had been left. The cattle now bawling and milling about in the woods were partly from the wild herd and partly from the tame one. With thousands of head of cattle roaming the countryside, this was how the Texas stockmen of those days built up the size of their herds.

After about an hour of circling, the riders closed in tightly on the herd, and gradually headed them out of the woods and toward the corral. They narrowed the herd down as they drew near the fence wings, until at last they passed through the gate into the corral. As the last one went inside, men were ready to close the gates and fasten them with strong poles.

"So that's a wild cattle hunt," Jim thought. He looked down at his clothes. There were a number of tears, and he still had cactus thorns stuck into his trousers. "I guess I'd better learn more about cattle drives. No one else seems to be such a mess."

Mr. Longworth saw him trying to pull together his

ripped shirt and trousers. He said, "Boy, you'd better get some chaps and a brush jacket. That's why the Mexicans wear them. Leather lets the thorns and brush slip over it without catching."

"Thanks, Mr. Longworth, I'll see about getting some," Jim said.

Longworth said nothing for a moment. Then he said, "You know, Cook, I almost didn't take you along on this drive."

"Why? Because I didn't have the right clothes?"

"No. Because when you interfered with my killing of that beef the other day I saw you were still a fool kid not dry behind the ears. I figured you might pull some dad-gummed show-off stunt and start a stampede today. Congratulations on behaving yourself."

Jim stared after his boss. It looked as if he had made an enemy. The men had already told him how easy it was to start a stampede. Sometimes so small a thing as a sneeze could startle the wild beef animals. It was a good thing no stampede had been started that day, or Jim knew he would have been blamed.

The wild cattle were kept in the corral with a few of the decoys for several days so that when they were given freedom they would be more interested in finding good grazing and water than in running wild. During those days, Jim's Mexican friends were teaching him how to handle a rope. He practiced on posts at first, until he felt he was ready to lasso an animal.

His new friends also helped him make a pair of leather *chaparajos,* or chaps, as the American cowboys called them. Worn over the trousers, they let a man ride through thorns and brush without ripping his clothing. One of the Mexicans gave him a brush jacket for the same purpose. It was a short jacket, made of tightly-woven cloth.

Before long, Jim had a chance to show that he had learned the art of roping. On a moonlit night, some of the cattle had become scattered. Each man rode after one of the animals. He was to rope it and hold it captive until the signal came to herd the animals together.

Jim found his "cow brute" and tied it down.

"I'm beginning to feel like a cowboy worth his salt," he thought as he climbed back into the saddle, after snugging up his rope.

In a few minutes, he heard the sound of cattle lowing, but it came in a human voice. This sound was often made by the Mexican cowboys as they chased an animal. Another cowboy, hearing the sound would know what was going on, but the noise would not bother other cattle.

"Maybe I can help this fellow," Jim thought, as the sound of the lowing came nearer. He moved off the trail, behind a clump of cactus.

He got his spare rope ready, with a loop in one end, and the other end tied to the saddle horn. Eagerly, he waited. In a few seconds, along came a young bull, shining black in the moonlight.

As the bull dashed past, Jim threw the loop over its head, making a perfect throw. He held on as the bull charged onward, waiting for the moment of the rope's tightening.

It came. The young bull, charging ahead full force, gave such a jolt that the cinch strap around Jim's pony broke. Saddle, Jim, with his feet still in the stirrups, and all went flying into the air. With a thud, Jim landed on his head while the saddle went bounding along behind the maddened bull. The cowhand, riding up a moment later, found that his horse was too winded to ever catch up with the escaping bull. He came back to help Jim, who was just beginning to see the real stars in place of those inside his head.

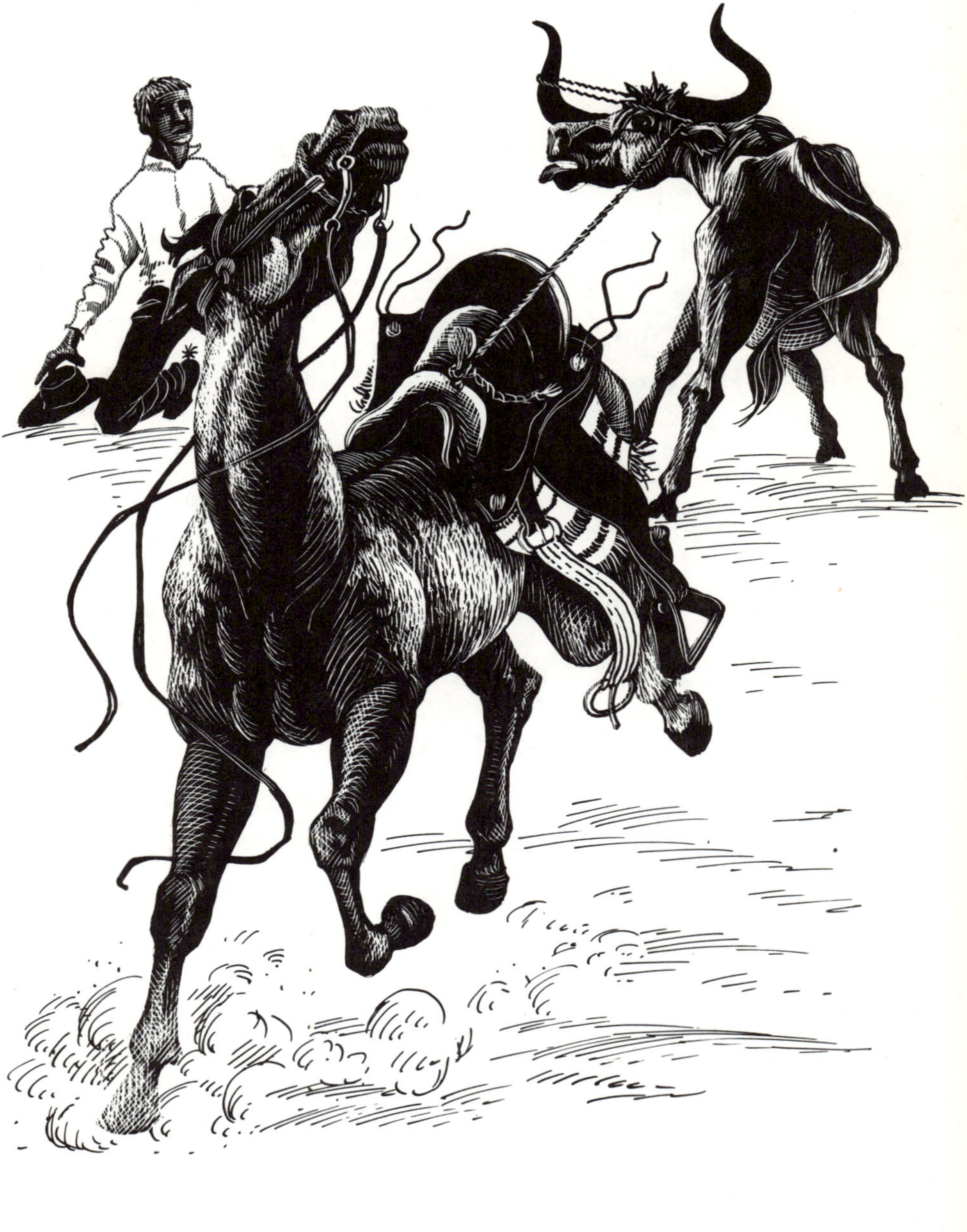

"*Es lástima, amigo,*" he said. Jim understood this to mean, "Too bad, my friend." He grinned and got to his feet with the Mexican's help. His horse stood waiting, saddleless. His rifle, which had flown from the saddle holster, lay not far away. He decided that he had no broken bones, but a "goose egg" was rising on his head.

"I'm sorry I made you lose your bull," he told the Mexican. "I guess I'm not as good a cowhand as I thought I was."

The Mexican grinned. "*No comprendo,*" he said.

Jim smiled in return. "*No importa,*" he said. "*Gracias, amigo.*"

He pulled himself onto his horse's back, aching almost too much to do it. The life of a cowboy was not the easy job he had thought it would be, he decided, feeling the lump rising on his head.

Mr. Longworth was not as forgiving as the other cowboy had been. It was not long after that that Longworth blamed Jim for a small stampede, and it was plain the two could never be friends.

GREENHORN ON THE CHISHOLM

Things grew worse between Mr. Longworth and Jim Cook. When spring came Jim felt he wanted to work for another boss, and asked Mr. Slaughter if he could go along with Mr. Roberts' crew on a cattle drive up the Chisholm Trail to Abilene, Kansas. About three thousand head of cattle bearing the T-Diamond brand were to be driven the eight-hundred miles to the railroad there. From Abilene they would be shipped east to Chicago or St. Louis.

Mr. Slaughter said, "Well, Jim, you're just getting to be a pretty good hand at catching wild cattle. Now you want to go off being a trail waddie. If you go up there, you won't come back, after I've spent a lot of time and money making a cowhand out of a green farm boy."

Jim said, "I promise, Mr. Slaughter — as soon as we get the cattle up to Abilene, I'll head right back here."

"We'll see what Joe Roberts has to say," said Mr. Slaughter.

Joe was pleased. "They tell me you can shoot a rabbit's eye at every pop. Now, if you are sure you can ride for four months without a single whole night's sleep, and will use that sharp eye with a gun to keep Indians from stealing our horses, I can use you. Be ready to roll out with us at sun-up."

So Jim stowed the pair of blankets and one change of clothing he was allowed to take along in the supply wagon, checked his ammunition and sharpened up his Bowie knife. His string of five horses was put with the *remuda,* as the horse herd was called, and he reported to Joe Roberts on time.

Roberts said, "Jim, you and Frank Dennis will ride herd on the horses for most of this drive. And remember, the drive can't go on without horses."

"Roll out!" was the call a moment later, and the wagon moved ahead right behind Joe Roberts. Jim and Frank Dennis, an older cowhand whom Jim admired, started the horse herd moving right behind the wagon. Next came the point men, at the head of the big cattle herd. The other "waddies" were placed around the herd so that at any point where an animal might stray, one of them could quickly circle out around the animal and force it to go back to the herd.

Roberts was soon out of sight. It was his job to locate the camping grounds where the herd could have water. Since the herd moved very slowly, he did not go many miles ahead. Soon he was back, telling the cook, who was also an expert ox-team driver, where the wagon would be stationed for the night.

The cattle bawled and milled around a great deal that first day. They had not yet learned the pattern of the drive: that they would be kept walking all day, and as darkness came would be allowed to stop. When they had had water to drink and had grazed awhile, they all would be expected to lie down close together and rest for the night while cowhands rode around them. The men each had to ride for half of the night, and sleep the other half. For this first part of the drive, a dozen or so extra hands were along. When the herd had learned the habits of the drive, the extra men would go back to the ranch.

The chuck wagon, with the horse herd following, were at the camping ground well ahead of the cattle. Jim and Frank hobbled the horses so that they could walk but could not gallop. Then they were free to go back to the chuck wagon and see how the cook was coming along.

"What's it going to be tonight?" Jim asked. He was a growing boy, and the hours between meals seemed too long to him.

"Cookie" had lowered the table-end of the wagon after getting a fire started.

"Steaks tonight," he said. "Sourdough biscuits, coffee — 'tain't like the Hotel Ritz, boy. No Fancy Dan hummingbird tongues here."

Jim rested awhile, watching the cook put chunks of suet into a big black Dutch oven and get it sizzling over a fire. So that it would heat a whole row of Dutch ovens, the fire was built in a shallow trench. While the fat sizzled, Cookie sliced chunks of beef, pounded them with the edge of an old saucer to make them more tender, salted the chunks and rolled them in flour, and then started them cooking. Into another Dutch oven went the sourdough biscuits. When the giant coffee pot was on the fire, too, the cook could take it easy for a little while until the men started coming in for supper.

About sundown, the herd arrived at the meadow Roberts had chosen for them. While half the men rode around them, the other half came into camp for supper, changing their saddles to fresh horses before they sat down to eat. Each man always kept a saddled horse ready near the camp, just in case there should be a stampede.

Joe Roberts came over to Jim. "As soon as you've finished eating, Jim, go out and ride herd on the cattle. They're restless tonight because they haven't learned yet what is expected of them."

Jim grinned. "Seems the cattle have to learn, same as we greenhorn trail waddies."

"That's about it, boy. And mind you don't do anything to stampede them. Even a skittish pony can start them running first night out. Take your gentlest horse, and ride slow and easy."

"Yes, sir," said Jim. He finished his last biscuit and swallowed his coffee. The cook made it strong enough to keep any cowhand awake for his hours on watch. "If a horseshoe will sink in it, it's too weak," was the guide.

The moonlight was bright enough so that Jim had no trouble seeing the herd, still grazing and milling about restlessly. As Jim took his place in the great circle of riding men, some of the animals dropped to the knees of their forelegs and with a grunt and a sigh let their bodies sink to the ground. The field began to take on a strange look, with all those pairs of longhorns picking up the glint of the moonlight.

But there was one old black cow that did not want to stay with the herd and settle down. She kept walking away from it. Frank Dennis, riding just ahead of Jim, was losing patience with her.

"Every hand has had to turn her back into the herd," he said, as he and Jim once more turned the cow back. "She thinks she's something special. Likely was some family's milk cow at one time."

Frank rode on, Jim a short distance behind him. Jim could hear the next cowhand, a Mexican, speaking softly in Spanish to the old cow. The voice was gentle, but Jim had learned enough Spanish now to know that the words were not. But all the swearing the cowhands did made no difference to old Mrs. Cow. She finally dropped to her knees and lay down to rest, but not with the herd. She stayed about thirty yards out. Rather than start the fuss again, the cowhands widened their circle to ride around her.

Quiet — deep, deep quiet — came then. The men who had been riding longest went to camp to rest for a few hours, and those left riding herd were farther apart. Often Jim could not see Frank, still riding in the place ahead of him. Darkness came as the moon sank low in the west.

Jim was bored. The small noises of saddle leather creaking under him, the newness of herd riding, even the strong coffee he had had with his supper were not enough to keep him alert. To have something to do and to help him keep awake, he made a game of seeing how close he could ride to the old black cow without disturbing her.

At each round, he came a little closer. At two feet, the old cow still did not even flick her ear. Three rounds later, the horse's hoofs almost touched her, and the cow did not even open her eyes.

"Wonder what she would do if I touched her as I rode by?" Jim thought. "I'll bet that wouldn't even make her twitch a muscle."

As he drew near the next time, he reached out with his foot, leaning to one side in his saddle, and touched the cow's neck. Quick as a wink, so suddenly that Jim nearly fell from the saddle, the cow was on her feet, giving a loud snort as she arose. She instantly swung toward the sleeping herd and plunged in among them.

"Moo-OOO--OO-UH! Moo-AWW-UH! M-M-M-MOOO-UNH!"

The bellowing grew into a roar, and the sound of hoofs on the ground beat out an accompaniment. The herd was in full stampede.

"Oh, my gosh! I've done it now!" Jim thought. He rode in the direction the herd had moved, heading into the brush beyond the meadow. He heard the shouts of the men now and then. They soon began their lowing sounds as they tried to calm the running animals, but there was still much crashing in the brush. Cattle and horses ran on in the darkness.

For some time, Jim rode aimlessly in the woods, his stomach turning inside out. What would he do now? Mr. Roberts had warned him, and still he had not had enough sense to be careful. He dreaded the moment when Joe would ask him about how the stampede started. Maybe — maybe they all knew already. Maybe Joe was gunning for him right now, as Longworth had done the time Jim accidentally ran a wild bull into the herd and started a much smaller stampede. That could happen to any cowhand, even an old one, but this time it was a boy's foolishness that caused it. Jim wondered if he should ride away now, never to be seen in Texas again.

Just then he rode near a Mexican cowhand.

"What happened?" Jim asked.

The cowhand said, "Stampede."

"I know," said Jim, "but what started it?"

"*Quien sabe?*" said the cowboy. He rode off on the trail of another escaping animal.

"Who knows? I do, that's who," Jim muttered. But he decided not to run away, since word had not yet spread.

Jim was lucky. Mr. Roberts decided it was just first night nervousness that started the stampede, and did not question the waddies. One of the few fences then in Texas had stopped the stampede, and made it possible for the riders to close in on the greater part of the herd. About five hundred cattle escaped. Mr. Roberts sent back to the ranch for replacements for them.

Jim carried his guilty secret with him. He had learned his lesson, and became as careful as an old cowhand, no longer playing "kid" games. But just the same, his conscience bothered him, and he longed for a chance to do something to make up for the loss he had caused.

About a week later, the herd reached the open, rolling plains and was out of the brush country. The extra hands turned back, and the herd, now wise in the ways of the Chisholm Trail, plodded on, day after long day. Life seemed too dull until the day that Joe Roberts came up to Jim with warnings to be on the alert for an Indian attack on the horse herd.

INDIANS ON THE CHISHOLM

"Indian sign around. Likely they'll try to take our horses in the night, Jim. From here on, you and Frank are off cattle riding. You will each spend half the night riding around the horse herd."

"Don't we hobble them any more?" Jim asked.

"Yes, we'll go on hobbling them. But Indians could crawl up in the night, cut hobbles and be away with the horses. Or they might stampede the *remuda* so badly that the animals break the hobbles."

One night they camped on a little creek that ran into the Llano River, in central Texas. Jim was riding the first half of the night. Frank was to take over when the other cowhands changed shifts in the night. As Jim herded the horses not far from the camp, he noticed that the animals were unusually restless.

Mr. Roberts noticed it, too. He walked over to talk to Jim. "Those horses know there are Comanches around. This may be the night they'll try to take the herd, Jim. I want you to take the herd out of this open meadow into the clearing in the middle of that cedar brake."

Jim was almost as nervous as the horses. He had never been in an Indian raid.

"But, Mr. Roberts," he said. "If I go in there, with those thick cedars all around me, I won't be able to see them coming. I'll be trapped. They could pick me off with one arrow and take all the horses without anyone in camp knowing what was happening."

Roberts' voice sharpened. "Look, boy, when did you get your know-how in Indian fighting? Now do what I say. In the open, they'd run off the horses and kill you, too. At least they can't run the horses as easily, or even see the herd, in that cedar brake."

"Yes, sir," said Jim. Roberts and another man helped him drive the remuda into the cedar brake. Then Jim was left alone to keep them there.

It was a toss-up as to which was more nervous, Jim or the horses. He rode quite fast in circling them partly to keep them from moving out and partly because he felt less like a target for an Indian arrow when he was moving fast. The camp was only about seventy-five yards away, but he felt as alone as if it were seventy-five miles.

At last, after what seemed many hours, he heard the man return from the cattle herd to awaken the new shift. Frank Dennis would be coming out to relieve him now. By peering through the trees, Jim could see the campfire, and after a while Frank's form was silhouetted against it. Logs had been tossed on it to help warm up the men, for it was a cold night.

Frank came riding out toward the cedar brake with a blanket wrapped around himself, Indian style. As he came into the open place in the middle of the cedar brake, Jim said, "You'll have to ride fast, Frank. They are hard to hold tonight."

"Stay a minute, Jim," Frank said. "I looked at the fire, and I can't make out a thing in the darkness."

Jim rode a few more times around the herd. When Frank called out, "Thanks, Jim, I can see the horses now," he gladly left the cedar brake and headed for the campfire.

He still had his rifle in his hand as he stopped his horse and stepped down in front of the blazing fire. As he did so, there came the sound of shots. Jim looked toward the cedar brake and saw some flashes. The attack had come!

Quickly, Jim raised his rifle and fired in the direc-

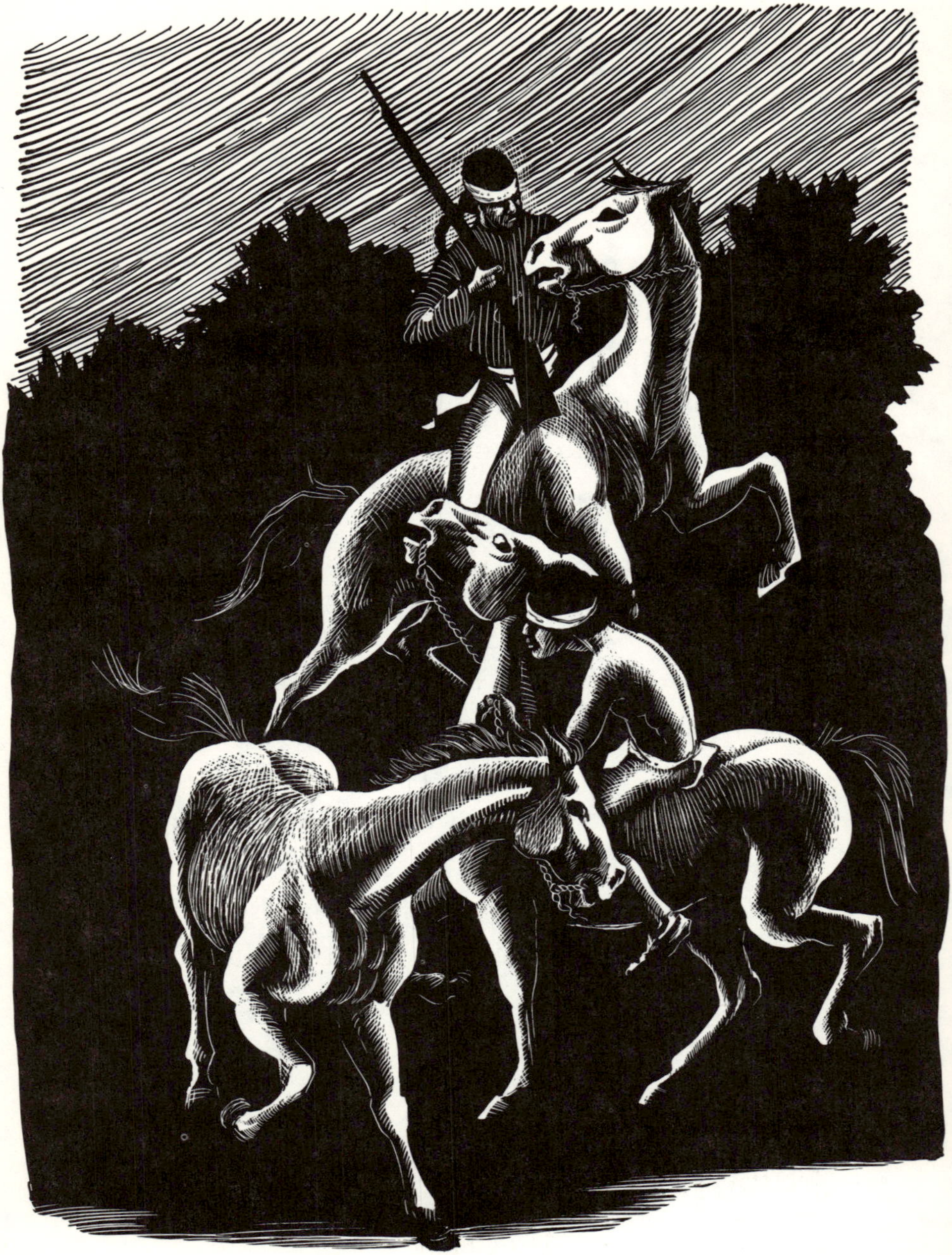

tion of the flashes. At the gunfire, the horse, too, had swung around, and boy and horse stood silhouetted. There was another flash, and a moment later the horse fell at Jim's feet, struck between the eyes by a bullet. Instantly, Jim dropped to the ground, crawling away from the firelight. He made his way to a big cedar tree whose branches grew close to the ground.

As he reached cover, he heard the sounds of pounding hoofs and crashing tree limbs. Stampeding, the horses were heading right through the camp. Neighing their fright, they tore through the camp as men ran to escape being trampled. Some charged against the rope that ran from the wagon wheels to some trees, to help hold horses. Over went the wagon and the rope snapped.

The horses picketed around the camp, saddled and ready for just such an emergency as this, broke loose in fright and joined the runaways. They headed toward the cattle herd, which instantly stampeded also, heading into cedar brakes. The bellowing of cattle and whinnying of horses, the pounding of hoofs and the crashing of branches made a roar in which were lost any sounds the Indians might be making.

Silence came to the camp as the animals and cowhands on duty galloped away. Joe Roberts called out, "Where are you, boys? Don't let them get away with all our horses! Come on, boys, after them!"

But the only horses left were those already being ridden. There was little the men could do on foot. When Jim came out from under the tree, he looked around for Frank Dennis. No one had seen him. Jim shivered. Frank probably lay dead back in that cedar brake. But for a few moments of time, Jim himself would have been the one.

About daylight, some of the men came in, bringing with them a few of the horses they had been able to stop. The cattle stampede had been stopped about a half mile away, but the Indians got away with most of the horses and some of the cattle. Saddles were gone, too, from the backs of the horses that had been picketed in the camp. As some of the men were getting ready to ride out bareback, Jim decided to go into the cedar brake to find Frank's body. As he started out, there was Frank, riding toward him.

"Good morning, boys!" he called out. "We had a very pleasant night of it, didn't we?"

He grinned, but as he got down from his horse, the

blood on his clothing could be seen. He had tied his neckerchief around his left hand. His blanket and saddle had several bullet holes in them, the saddle horn was completely shot away. An arrow still was stuck between the back of the saddle and the saddle blanket. The horse was limping, with blood caked on one of his legs.

Frank told his story. "They were just inside the woods, not more than fifteen feet from me when they blazed away. Likely they heard us talking, Jim. I made a big target with that blanket around me, and they thought they had killed me. I rode after them as long as I could — they headed the herd off toward that canyon yonder."

Immediately, some of the men headed for the canyon. There, now feeding quietly, were about three-fourths of the missing horses, for the Indians had been forced to leave them when they heard the cowboys coming, for fear of being boxed in the canyon. The men rounded up the horses and brought them back.

The men were beginning to feel better, then, even though they knew it would be uncomfortable riding without saddles until they could reach a supply station. About ten o'clock, two buffalo hunters came walking into the camp.

"You fellows seen any Indians with our horses?" they asked. "We had ten of them, and they were run off in the night."

Roberts said, "I wish we had lost only ten."

"How about helping us round them up?" the hunters asked. "If you will lend us some horses to ride, and let a few of your men come along, maybe we can get most of the horses back."

Jim, listening, thought of the night he had caused the stampede. Here was a chance to do something to help make up for it. He listened for Mr. Roberts' answer.

"Well, we can't start out on the trail today anyway. If there are three men willing, they may go for a day or two and give it a try."

"I'll go, Mr. Roberts," Jim said. He didn't notice the look the buffalo hunters gave him. He forgot that he was still a slim boy of fourteen, rather small for his age.

But Mr. Roberts saw the look. "Jim Cook is the best shot I have. He'll be a good one to go along," he said, and the hunters looked more pleased. Two other men offered, and soon the five were on horseback, on their way to the buffalo hunters' camp. There they picked up the trail of the horses stolen from the hunters.

"A few of our horses had shoes," one of the hunters said. He pointed out the tracks of the shod ponies. "These tracks should take us to the Indian camp."

They did. By evening, the men had found it. The camp was in a valley near a spring, with hills on three sides. From the top of a hill, the men could see the stolen horses, picketed near the camp. They took their five horses to a thicket and hid them well. Then they went back to the hilltop to watch, planning to wait for daylight.

"We'll go to the hill over on the other side," the buffalo hunters said. "We'll take this little camp easily. I'll bet the young bucks are out stealing more horses. Can't see any of them in camp."

As dawn's light came to the hilltops, an old Indian began to walk from the camp toward the hill where the cowhands waited. One of the cowboys fired, bringing the man down. Instantly, the Indian camp came to life. In a moment, a brave was on his pony and charging up the hill toward the cowboys. From the farther hill, a bullet from one of the buffalo hunters' big guns came across toward the Indian.

It came nearer to Jim than to the Indian. The boy crouched low, aiming his rifle at the oncoming Indian, who was off to one side of him now. He fired, just as the rider and his pony charged past.

"Got him," he muttered, but it was the horse and not the rider he had struck. Down went the pony, but the Indian, gun in hand, charged on over the hilltop. Jim shouted back to his companions, "Don't shoot me! I'm going down to the camp for the horses!"

He half ran, half slid down the slope. The horses were tied in a clump of willows near the stream that ran from the spring. Jim quickly slashed tethers to free the animals, seeing that the others had followed him and were ready to help herd the animals. One of the cattlemen's horses was still saddled. Jim jumped onto the horse's back, as each of the others chose a horse to ride also. Some were carrying Indian saddles. A number of the cattlemen's saddles were seen in the camp slashed to bits.

Not an Indian came to stop them, but the men wasted no time. At a gallop, they herded the horses out of the valley. They stopped only to get the five horses they had hidden the night before, and then went back to the hunters' and cattlemen's camps. Camp was

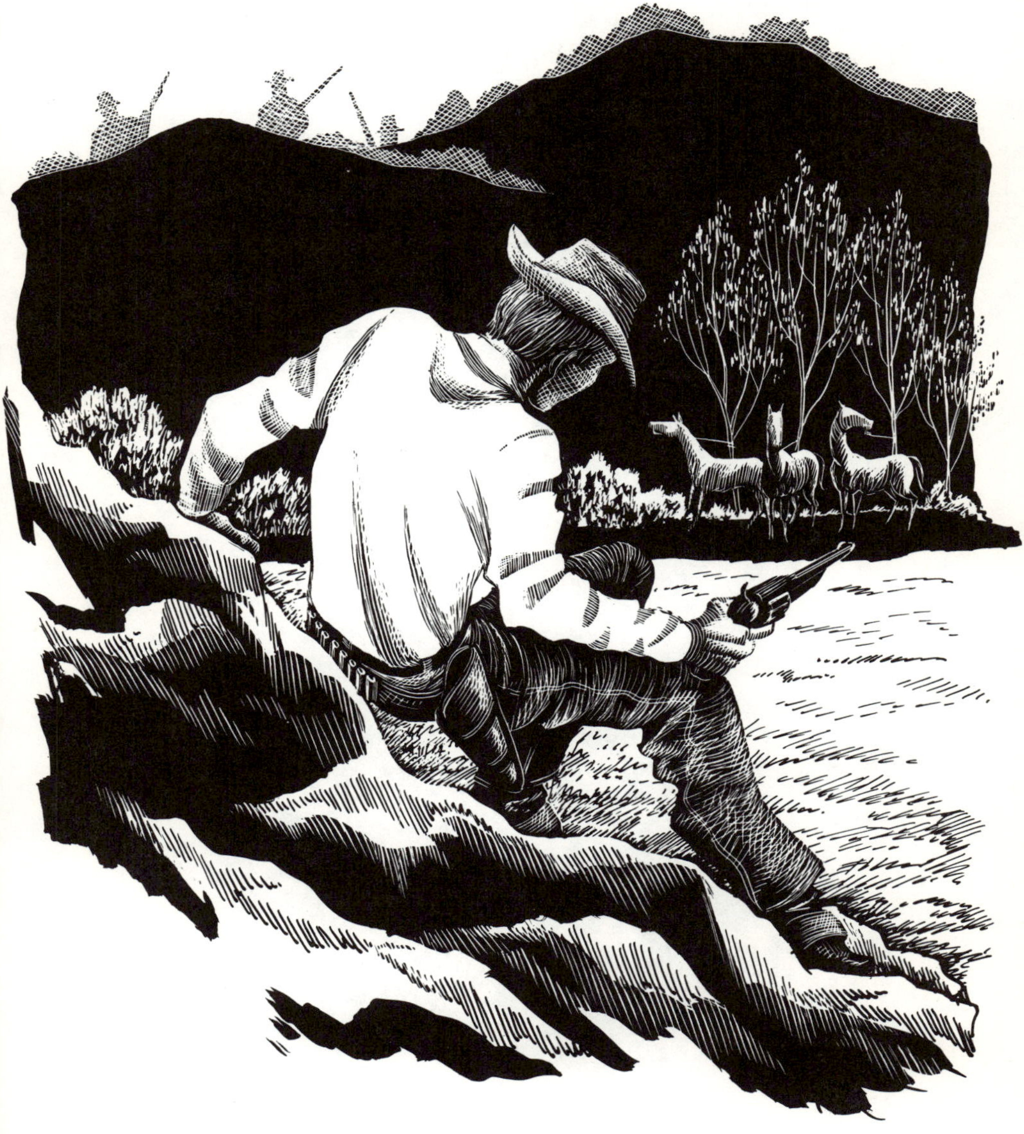

broken as soon as they returned, so that distance could be put between them and the Indians. The herds were well on their way before darkness came to this spot that had been the scene of so much trouble.

As he rode herd on the horses, Jim felt better. He had made up in a small way for his earlier foolishness.

Jim Cook kept the secret of how that stampede started for fifty years. Then as he was growing old, after becoming a rancher himself and learning the cattle business completely, he wrote a book. In it he told the story of his greenhorn days on the Chisholm Trail.

Tom Smith's Story

TRAIL'S END MARSHALL

When drovers reached the end of the trail after the long months on horseback, they looked for a good time. Usually they found it in the saloons and dance halls that lined the main street of every town at a trail's end.

Abilene, like a number of other towns in Kansas, got its start as a railroad shipping point for cattle. When it was new, the people hoped to keep it a quiet, peaceful, business town. By the time Jim Cook got there, the town, though only three years old, had gone through its roughest days. From those rough days had come a hero, a quiet fellow named Tom Smith.

In 1869, the first year, the town council voted to build a jail across the street from Bull's Head Saloon on Texas Street. The little square stone building was almost finished on the night that a gang of cowhands came whooping and shouting out the doors of the Bull's Head.

"Whoopee! Let's tear down the jail!"

"Yahoo! Down she comes! Ain't nobody going to lock us up in Abilene!"

And in a few minutes, the stone walls were a heap of mortar and rock.

The councilmen met the next morning.

"There's just one thing to do to keep order in this town," said Mayor Henry. "We've got to pass a law against the carrying of firearms in town. We'll post signs saying every cowhand who comes to town must check his guns in the sheriff's office."

As men went to work to rebuild the jail, signs were posted. The Texas cowhands shot the signs full of holes, and the county sheriff couldn't get any of them to check their guns with him.

Mayor Henry called another meeting. "We've got to hire a town marshal," he said, and the councilmen agreed.

One of the first men to ask for the job was Tom Smith, who had worked on the railroads after he went west, and then had been marshal in a Wyoming town, and had been a good one.

Tom Smith rode down on his big gray horse, *Silverheels*. The councilmen liked him right away. He was strong and handsome, and yet rather boyish looking when he took off his hat and showed his thatch of redbrown hair. The men liked the thoughtful, honest look in Tom's eyes when he answered their questions. There was just one thing that bothered them.

Captain Shane, who was Mayor Henry's partner in their land office over on Buckeye Street, asked Tom Smith about it. "They tell me you are called 'Bear River Tom' because you were the leader in that battle against the sheriff up in the mountain country. Is that so?"

Tom's mouth tightened. "I reckon that is so, Captain Shane. I led the fight because I believed my side was in the right."

Shane shook his head. "That was a bad riot, Mr. Smith. Very bad. Word of it spread all over the West."

"Sometimes it takes strong action to bring about a change for the good," Tom Smith said. "That is what Abilene needs."

Mayor Henry arose. "Thank you, Mr. Smith. We will let you know what we decide."

When the trustees talked it over, they decided that perhaps Tom Smith was too much of a fighter for their little town.

"After all, we don't want Abilene to be thought of as a rough place. We want to be proud of our little city," said Captain Shane.

So Tom went away, and a young man of the town was chosen to be marshal. Nothing changed. The cowboys laughed at him. Then two men just out of the army were given the job. They arrested the cook of a cattle drive when he rode his horse through town, firing his gun. They locked him in the jail, and peace lasted until time for the next meal in the cowmen's camp.

Into town rode the herders. They shot the lock off the jail door and let out their cook. The two marshals were hiding behind a building, and made for the next train out of town as soon as they could. Abilene wasn't safe enough, even in broad daylight, for a woman to go to the general store to buy her groceries. Gunmen came from other places to get the cowboys into card games at which they would lose their money. Things grew worse and worse.

Mayor Henry called the councilmen together again. "Gentlemen, I think perhaps we need the strong action of which Bear-River Tom spoke. All those in favor of sending for him say 'Aye.' "

"Aye," said all the councilmen.

On a Saturday morning in late May, 1870, Tom Smith came riding back into Abilene. Mayor Henry told him of the town's troubles.

"Maybe you won't want the job now, Tom. Things are worse than ever. Look the town over today, and let me know if you think you can handle it."

Tom smiled grimly. He left the office. Near sundown, Mayor Henry saw him come striding back.

"Well, what do you think?" asked Mayor Henry.

"I can handle it," said Tom, and he was sworn in then and there.

"Guns and drunken cowboys don't mix," the new marshal said. "You've got a law about checking guns. I'm going to enforce it."

"Well, here we go again," thought Mayor Henry, but he shook Tom's hand and promised to get new signs made. He watched Smith walk away in the direction of Abilene's thirty-two saloons.

Tom hadn't been marshal of Abilene ten minutes when he met Big Hank, who thought of himself as a tough man, and always wore a holster with loaded pistols in it. Big Hank planted himself firmly in Marshal Smith's path.

"So, you're going to be our marshal and run the town, are you?" he said. His right hand rested on his gun handle.

"That's right," said Smith. "I must trouble you to

hand me your guns. Firearms are not to be carried inside the Abilene limits."

Big Hank swore.

Coolly, Smith repeated, "Hand me your guns, sir."

Big Hank's mouth opened to let out another stream of swear words, but only a few had come out when the jaw was clamped shut. Quick as lightning, Smith's right arm had struck out to catch Big Hank under the chin. He fell flat on his back. Smith quickly took his guns, and as Big Hank got to his feet, stood ready for whatever was to come.

Big Hank felt for his guns, but his holster was empty. Suddenly his courage was gone, with the guns. When Smith said, "Get out of town. Now!" Big Hank headed for his camp.

That Saturday night there was something new to talk about all up and down saloon row on Texas Street. Another tough man, Wyoming Frank, shouted out, "He won't take my gun away from me!"

Everyone turned to the boaster. "Let's see the fun, boys. Go try him, Frank!"

Frank wasn't quite ready. "I will," he said. "Soon as I'm ready."

"Now," said his pals. But Frank wanted to wait at

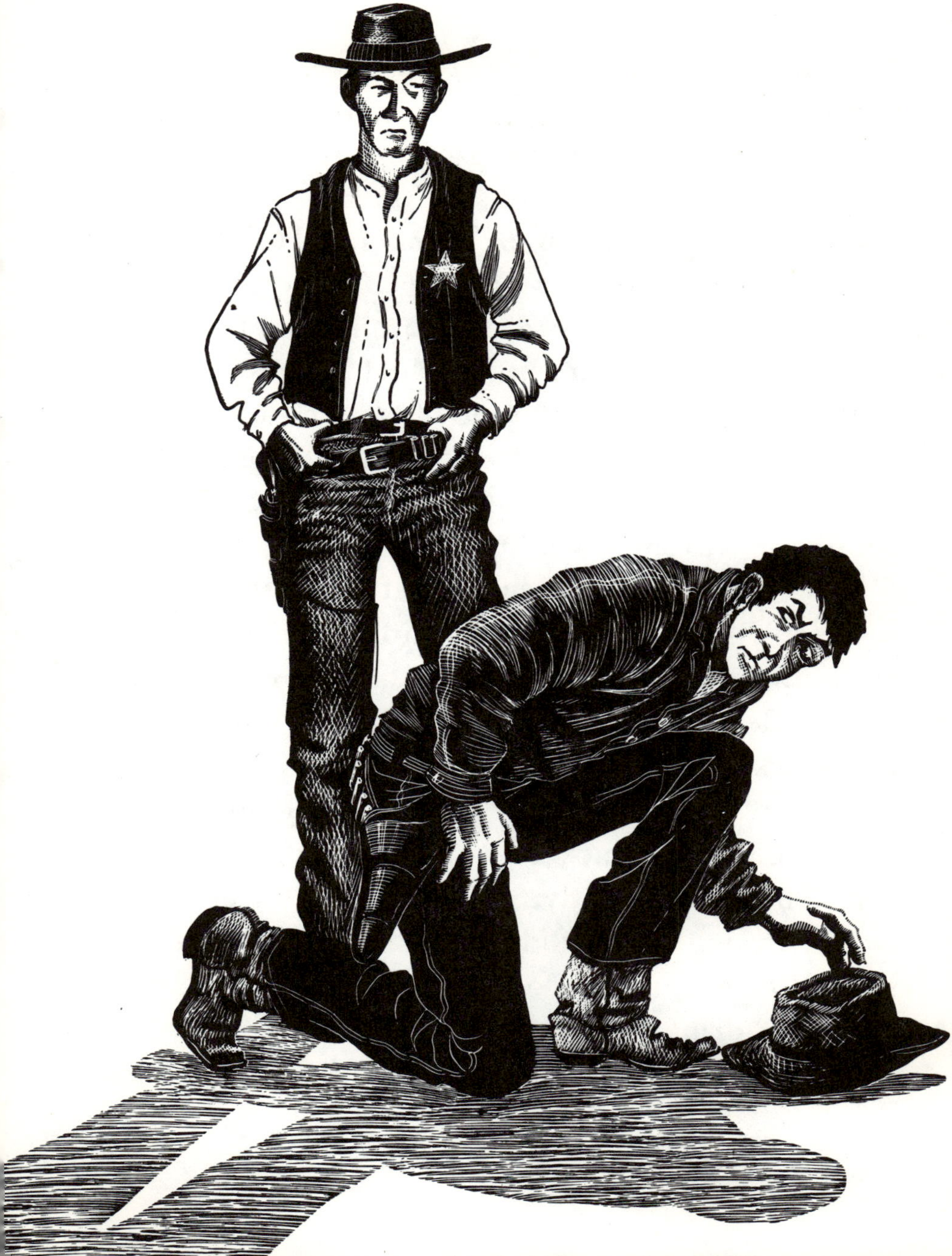

least until morning. They were all there watching him the next morning, Sunday, as he stood in Texas Street waiting for Marshal Smith to show up. An hour went by, and Tom did not appear. Frank went into the saloon then to do some more drinking. "He heard I was waiting for him, and he's lit out already, just like the other marshals," Frank said. He pulled out his revolver and polished it with his neckerchief. "Guess I might as well go tell the boys we got rid of another marshal."

He started up the dusty street, walking down the middle of it. But also walking in the middle of the street, coming toward him, was Marshal Tom Smith.

"Surrender your gun, sir," said the marshal.

"Who's going to make me? A tinhorn marshal?"

Smith knew that Frank would be on guard against a blow under the chin such as he had given Big Hank. He rested his hand on his own revolver handle, and kept walking closer and closer to Wyoming Frank, who finally began to back away. Smith would not draw first, but he was ready for the moment when Frank would draw. Frank did not reach for his gun, but backed right into the doorway of the saloon where he had been drinking.

Marshal Smith followed him inside. "Your gun,

please," he said and held out his hand.

Wyoming Frank heard one of his pals laugh. He swore. It was as if the sound of a swear word was a trigger in Marshal Smith's quick-moving body. Instantly he landed a blow, as Wyoming Frank was reaching for his gun. The gunshot went into the ceiling, and Frank was on his back on the floor. The watching men did not know it then, but their new marshal had once been a policeman in New York City, and was trained in catching a man off his guard.

Smith whipped off Wyoming Frank's holster after taking the revolver. He gave the gunman a few blows with the belt and then said, "Now get up on your feet. I'll give you five minutes to be out of this town, and don't ever let me set eyes on you again."

No one laughed now. Wyoming Frank got up without a word, found his hat, and slouched out. Marshal Smith's eyes were still blazing as he too turned and left the saloon.

As cattlemen rode into Abilene that summer, they watched for the handsome marshal on his big gray horse, and all of them made sure they were not wearing guns. Once again, ladies could walk to the grocery store. Somehow, everyone knew that Tom Smith was boss, even though he had never been seen drawing his gun, and spent most of his time riding up and down Texas Street on *Silverheels*.

Now and then a cattleman came into town not knowing about Tom Smith. One of them went into the Old Fruit Saloon, wearing his gun. He came out of the saloon slung over Tom's shoulder and wasn't put down until he was in the jail across from the Bull's Head down the street. His friends just stood by and watched, and this time no one tried to shoot the lock off the jail.

Peace lasted five months. Most of the cattlemen had already headed back for Texas on the day in November that Marshal Smith was asked to go out to a frontier sodbuster's farm where there had been a shooting. The sodbuster, Andrew McConnell, had found his neighbor driving cattle across his cornfield. The men drew guns on each other, and the neighbor had been killed. The sheriff had asked Tom Smith and his deputy to help with the arrest, even though it was outside of Abilene.

McConnell was inside his dugout, and refused to come out.

"You're under arrest, McConnell!" Smith called out. "Come out and save yourself a lot of trouble."

Still the man didn't come out. Smith called again,

and then said, "I'll have to go in for him."

He walked down the spaded out steps that led to the dugout door, opened the door and went in. He could see nothing at first, in the gloom of the dugout after the bright sunshine outdoors. By the time he could see where McConnell was, and that a second man was in the dugout with him, McConnell had his rifle aimed. He shot at Smith as the other man ran out to hold off the deputy.

Marshal Smith, badly wounded, fought with McConnell and forced him outside, only to be struck down with an ax by the other man. Two days later, *Silverheels* walked slowly behind a wagon carrying a coffin, his saddle empty and stirrups dangling. All of Abilene followed sadly.

Tom's short stay in Abilene had changed the town, and the people never forgot their hero. When Wild Bill Hickok came the next spring to be marshal, he had very little trouble. Soon the cattle shipping center had moved on farther west and south, to Dodge City, and Abilene could settle down to being a farming community. It was a quiet place and very peaceful twenty years later when a little boy, two-year-old Dwight Eisenhower, was brought there by his parents. The story of the little town at trail's end where our thirty-fourth President grew up is much like that of other "cow towns."

Will Rogers' Story

LATER DAY COWBOY

In those same twenty years when Abilene was settling down into a quiet farm shipping center, the old frontier ways were disappearing. Homesteaders and barbed wire blocked the way of the great herds of cattle. The railroads built branch lines down into the Texas ranch country, and there was no longer the need to trail the herds long distances.

On a ranch in Indian Territory, a part-Cherokee boy named Will Rogers was growing up in those years of change. But to him the world of the cowboy was the only world that mattered. From the time he could sit up and a cowhand on his father's ranch sat him on a pillow behind the saddle horn, he wanted to be on horseback riding the range.

As soon as he could walk, he was playing with a rope. The cowhands taught him simple rope tricks and cheered him on. His father bought a lively little pony for him, and while Willie's mother closed her eyes so that she wouldn't have to watch, the little fellow clung to the pony and learned to ride.

"Please be careful," his mother would say. Willie was her eighth child, but the only other boy who had lived beyond babyhood had died when Willie was two years old, and there were no more babies after Willie.

His father, Clem Rogers, was an important man in Cooweescoowee District where the Cherokee lands were located. He had started as a boy with a small herd of cattle and built it up to give him and his family a good living. By the time William Penn Adair Rogers was born, on November 4, 1879, Clem had been able to build a big, solid, two-story home. It was built of square-hewn walnut logs, covered over with white-painted siding, with the inside walls all plastered. Clem was made a judge of the district, and when it was time to form counties and a state, Rogers County of Oklahoma was named in his honor.

Willie was sent to the one-room log country school with the other Cherokee boys and girls, but it seemed to his father that he wasn't learning much except how to beat the other boys at running foot races. After a year or two, he was sent with one of his older sisters to a girls' boarding school, where he was to be company for the school president's son. There he seemed to learn more, including a love for singing that stayed with him always.

The second year, when he came home for vacation, Willie found that his mother was very sick. She died that summer, and ten-year-old Willie was heartbroken. Finally his father decided to send the boy to new surroundings to help him over the sadness. He went to school first in a nearby Indian Territory town, then, when he did not do well except in planning mischief, to another school. He was popular and made good grades when he chose to study, but his father was not pleased.

"Will," he told him, "I want you to settle down and begin to get ready for manhood. You need a good schooling to be a lawyer, or a doctor, or whatever you decide to be."

Will felt uncomfortable. "Dad, I want to be a cowboy. I don't need any more schooling."

Mr. Rogers said, "Son, the days of the big ranches are over. Look how mine has shrunk, and now it's used more for wheat than for cattle raising. No, you'll have to choose another way to make a living."

So off to another school, and then another, went Will Rogers. When he was seventeen, he was sent to Kemper Military Academy at Boonville, Missouri.

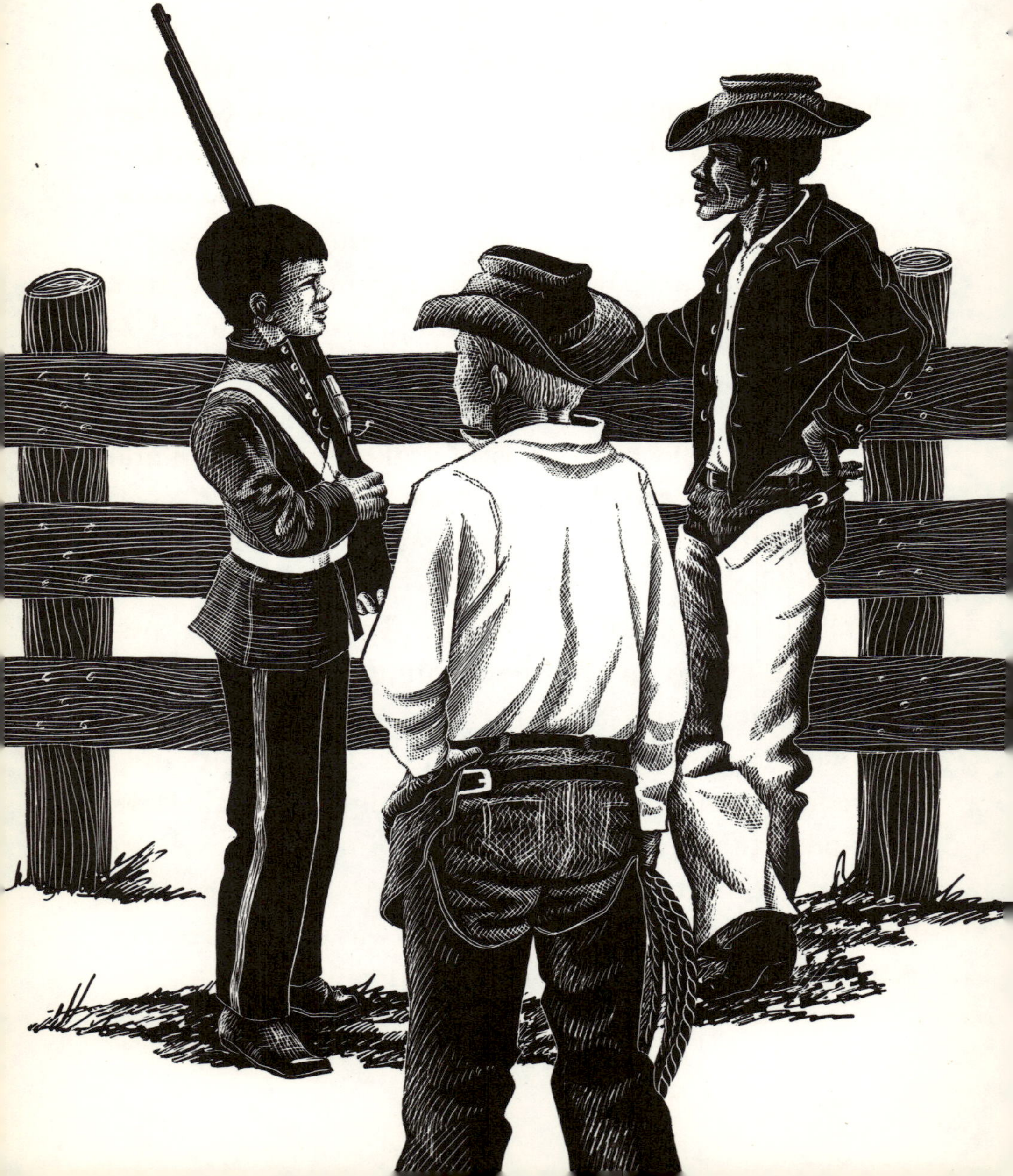

"I hope the military discipline will make you settle down," his father told him, and it seemed to at first. Will loved the uniform and the military drills. When he came home on vacation, he hurried out to the corral to show off for the cowhands.

"I'll show you the manual of arms," he said. "Let me take a rifle. Got to have a rifle to do it with."

One of the cowhands handed him his rifle, and smartly Will went through the drill. But he snapped the rifle butt to the ground too suddenly. The gun went off, grazing the boy's face and sending his hat flying into the air. He had a scar on his forehead the rest of his life from this narrow brush with death.

Near the end of the second year at Kemper, Will decided he just had to get back to ranching. He had a pal who was from the Texas "panhandle" and the two talked often of ranch life.

"That's where there are still wide-open spaces," the boys said.

Will wrote to his older sisters, asking each to send him ten dollars. With the money, he left Kemper as soon as the spring breezes began to blow. At Amarillo, Texas, he tried to get work, having bought an "outfit" for himself. The horse he could afford was cheap because it had eaten loco weed and was also getting old, but it was better than none. Soon he had a job on a ranch, and through the hot summer months, he worked seven long days a week, riding herd, roping and branding calves, and loving it.

When at last he went back home, his father saw it was no use sending Will back to school.

"If you're going to be a cattle man, I'll give you a small herd to start you off," he said. But it was plain to see he was disappointed.

But so was Will. Herding cattle on a small ranch was tame work by then, around the year 1900. He longed for the open-range, cattle-drive days that the older cowhands talked about.

"There's a new cattle frontier down in South America in Argentina," he heard in town. Nothing would satisfy Will short of going there. His herd was worth several thousand dollars by that time, and with a friend named Dick Parris, he made plans to sell out and head for Buenos Aires, Argentina. They went south to New Orleans and then to Galveston, Texas, looking for a ship sailing to South America.

"Better go to New York and ship out from there," the boys were told. Will had plenty of money, so they went to New York and saw the city for a couple of weeks. Still no ship was sailing for the Argentine.

"Go to London. Lots of trade between the British and the South Americans," they were advised. And that is what they did. It was late in March when they got to London. Ten days later, they were at last on board a ship headed for Buenos Aires. And Will Rogers was seasick every day of each of the sea voyages.

He said as they reached port at last, "Dick, no matter how badly I need work, don't ever let me sign on as a sailor!"

But that was almost exactly what he did. He and Dick were very disappointed in the cattle ranches of Argentina. Only the wealthy could own one of the giant ranches, and the cowboys were paid less than five dollars a week. Furthermore, Will and Dick felt that their working methods were not up to the skillful ways of Texas cowboys.

Dick wanted to go home, and Will used the last of his money to buy his pal a ticket, expecting Clem Rogers to send more money as he had done in past years. But Will's father had decided the boy was on his own, and sent none. Will was downhearted the day he went over to the stockyards and saw *gauchos* trying to rope wild mules. Seeing them miss time and again, the boy borrowed a rope and made one mule pull up short on his first throw.

"Twenty-five cents for each one you catch," the boss said.

While he was doing that he was given a chance to work at cattle tending on a ship taking livestock to South Africa. He wanted to head for home, but needed the job. Of course he got seasick immediately, and could hardly earn his way. But once in South Africa, the owner of the livestock on the ship hired him to help with horses and mules on his ranch.

He worked there until December. Then he was asked to drive a bunch of mules to the town of Ladysmith. On the way, he saw posters for Texas Jack's Wild West Show. Such shows had become popular all over the world, beginning with Buffalo Bill's show of the 1880's and 1890's, for all the world loved the riding, shooting, roping American cowboy.

Will could hardly wait to go to see Texas Jack and find out if he was really from Texas and above all, a true cowboy.

"Sure am," said Texas Jack. "And who are you?"

"My name is Will Rogers, and I'm a cowboy from Indian Territory," he said.

"Is that so? Are you pretty good at riding and roping?"

"Just fair as a rider, but I can handle a rope pretty well," said Will. He showed Texas Jack a little of what he could do, including the Big Crinoline, one of the most difficult tricks.

Then came the words that started Will Rogers on his career.

"How would you like a job in my show?"

He started right away. Billed as "The Cherokee Kid," he did riding and rope tricks. He worked his way around the world in such shows, finally getting back home just in time to take part in the show at the Louisiana Exposition, the World's Fair of 1904, in St. Louis.

Next it was vaudeville, in Chicago and then in New York. After he had stopped a panic in Madison Square Garden by roping a runaway steer in a Wild West Show, Will saw that people liked action as well as tricks in roping, and added a live pony to his theater act.

The first time he talked from the stage, Will didn't mean to be funny, and was hurt when people laughed at his Oklahoma drawl. But after a while, jokes and story telling went along with his rope tricks. He became the most famous cowboy in the United States. Between shows, he went to the fine California ranch he bought with the money he had earned. Even his father felt a little better about his wayward son by then, but Will told about some of his old neighbors from Oklahoma who came to see his show in New York.

When they got back home someone asked, "Well, what is Willie doing these days?"

"Still playing the fool, same as always."

But to the President of the United States, who saw the movies in which Will played and read the humorous comments on the day's news that he wrote for a large group of daily newspapers, Will Rogers was not a fool. President Coolidge sent Will to Europe in 1926 as his personal "ambassador of good will."

Will Rogers met death a few years after that, flying with a famous pioneer aviator, Wiley Post, in the days of the one-engine planes. The plane fell as it crossed Alaska. All America and much of the world felt the loss of this later-day cowboy who could spin a yarn and a rope at the same time and make people see the humor in everyday happenings.

Now the old-time cowboys are gone, and the trails

they followed are remembered only by the markers here and there on the great highways that cross them now. But the cowboy will always be remembered. His days and ways make a colorful chapter in the story of America's frontiers.

Edith McCall, in her *Frontiers of America* books, writes in simple uncluttered text without losing the dramatic impact of her true stories of real people. Her purpose is to make these stories of our country available to younger readers and still vital and interesting to a wide age range.

Mrs. McCall now lives in the Ozarks and writes for children. For many years, she was a reading consultant in LaGrange, Illinois.

Carol Rogers, illustrator of this book, lives in the country outside of Austin, Texas, where she spends part of each week clambering up and down canyons and through cedar breaks mending fences. Every time she goes to town she drives over a part of the Chisholm Trail.